# THE
# PERFECT
# FRANCHISE

### Build wealth,
### achieve freedom,
### & live your dream life

## MARK SCHNURMAN

# DEDICATION

*To my parents, who taught me how to love, laugh, and cry.*

*You showed me how to live an imperfectly perfect life.*

# ACKNOWLEDGEMENT

This book would not be possible without my wife Lisbeth. She provided me with the time to write and helped to refine the book. Importantly, she took out my Montaigne quote (that did not belong) and my references to the movie Vision Quest.

Thanks to Vicki Greer who worked with me to edit the book.

# STYLE NOTE FOR THE READER

One thing you will quickly learn about me is that my style and approach are informal and personal. I want to connect with you on an authentic, human level. With that as the foundation, I will speak in the first person and use the pronouns "I" and "you" where possible. The term "client" is used when referring to my particular franchise consulting clients when "you" is not appropriate. Finally, the term candidate is used to refer to prospective franchisees in general.

# CONTENTS

# INTRODUCTION

*"Your life does not get better by chance;*
*it gets better by change."*

—Jim Rohn, entrepreneur

I hope you are wondering what makes me an expert on franchising.

Why?

Because that is the exact question you should be asking right now.

The simple answer is that the experiences in my career—both inside and outside the franchise community—uniquely position me to help you explore business and franchise ownership.

Consider the following.

First, my career has been focused on developing people and companies. I know what makes both succeed; I know what causes both to fail. I have experience hiring, training, managing, and placing thousands of people.

I have strong corporate, coaching, business ownership, and franchising experience. While I was building companies, I ran a small career-coaching practice, taught human resources at Penn State University, and authored a career advice column in the *Star-Ledger,* New Jersey's largest newspaper.

As a franchisee, I understand firsthand the benefits of franchising. A few years ago, I started helping people explore franchise ownership. Now I am one of the top franchise consultants in the country and a member of the prestigious Forbes Business Council. My extensive and diverse experience allows me to quickly understand situations, assimilate information, and guide you.

There is a difference between wisdom and smarts. Wise people learn from the mistakes of others. Smart people learn from their own mistakes. I want you to share in the wisdom that I have accumulated through mistakes and successes, trial and error. The setbacks I experienced helped me become who I am and enable me to assist you in a way that many cannot.

Further, I am systems oriented, and the franchise exploration process I employ has resulted in thousands of successful and happy franchisees. The approach is simple. It will enable you to decide if franchising is the right path and identify your best brand match.

In addition, I facilitate a robust due diligence and provide insider insights that you will not find anywhere else. This is important because without them, it is easy to make mistakes. Franchising is not about hot or sexy brands. Franchising is about finding the right match for your unique goals, objectives, talents, and financial situation.

Finally, I keep you focused on your goals and help you understand whether a specific franchise can help you achieve them. Your objective is to identify a franchise brand that works best for you.

So, are you committed to working for the next 90–120 days to find the right fit? If so, I can help you learn, explore, and decide on whether franchising is right for you!

My commitment to you, and to my franchise-consulting clients, is that if business ownership makes sense, I will advocate to make it a reality. It is both wonderful and life changing! However, while business ownership is a great option for many, it is not right for everyone. In fact, I advise almost half of the candidates I speak with that franchising is not a good option for them on our first call.

**Business Ownership and The American Dream**

Americans are a uniquely wonderful people. We are hardworking, creative, and independent. We strive to achieve the American Dream—professional success, a family, a house, and a better quality of life than our parents. A large part of the American Dream is being your own boss. In fact, over two-thirds of Americans believe that entrepreneurship and business ownership are fundamental parts of the American Dream. If you are reading this book, you are almost certainly part of that group. Yet only about 15 percent of us become business owners.

What accounts for the disparity between our dreams and realities? There are numerous factors that conspire to keep you tethered to working for others, eschewing your dreams.

First, while the majority of us want to be our own bosses, many of us lack the compelling idea for a business. In many cases, even if we do possess an exciting idea, we lack the business acumen and capability to create a turnkey system that can ensure success. There is good news. Franchising can provide you the brand, business model, and the support to facilitate success as a business owner.

The second reason we fail to follow our dreams is that we are afraid. Fear expands when we venture outside of our comfort zones. Fear can cause you to lose sight of what is important to you and what you want to achieve. Good news: Franchising provides a clear process to overcome your fears, launch a business, and realize your dreams.

That is what this book is about. On the following pages, you will be introduced to the world of franchising, and provided the tools to navigate the inevitable emotional challenges of starting a business.

The seminal truth in franchise selection is to follow the process. It sounds simple, but in truth it is hard. People can become enamored with a shiny, faddy new brand that makes no sense for them, and shun a great concept fit too quickly. Be patient. The process works!

If you join a franchise, you will experience a change. Change is difficult because people exaggerate the importance of what they have or are already doing. We become attached to things we have and that, once again, makes them more valuable to us.

Survey after survey shows that most careers are defined by low levels of satisfaction. When we accept less than is possible, we wallow in mediocrity. You can have a great career and a great life. You just need to choose great over middling or good enough. Change takes effort and has risk. Again, do not let good or okay mute your drive and catalyst to change. Do not let fear limit you.

You can break the pattern and live the life you have imagined. You can be your own boss. It starts with courage and an open mind. I help people do it every single day.

You deserve to be inspired, fulfilled, and full of passion. I am not talking about being satisfied or happy. You can go to a job, finish a project and feel happy or relieved. That is transitory. Harry Chapin, the great singer-songwriter, tells a story about his grandfather that elucidates this point. Relating the story from his grandfather, Chapin said,

"Harry, there are two kinds of tired: there's good tired, and there's bad tired. Ironically enough, bad tired can be a day that you won. But you won other people's battles; you lived other people's days, other people's agendas, other people's dreams. And when it's all over, there was very little you in there. And when you hit the hay at night, somehow you toss and turn; you don't settle easy."

He said, "Good tired, ironically enough, can be a day that you lost. But you don't even have to tell yourself because you knew you fought your battles, you chased your dreams, you lived your days, and when you hit the hay at night, you settle easy—you sleep the sleep of the just, and you can say 'take me away.'" He said, "Harry, all my life I've wanted to be a painter and I've painted; God, I would've loved to be more successful, but I painted and I painted and I'm good tired and they can take me away."

When I launched my consulting business, I did not do a lot of winning. In fact, for the first time in my professional career, I was getting my butt kicked every single day. I had a lot to learn and was drinking from a fire hose.

But I felt invigorated and deeply motivated. Every night I was satisfied. Every morning I was excited. I fought to learn more. I fought to grow. I fought to succeed. I was in the battle.

I was the man in the arena Teddy Roosevelt was speaking about. "It is not the critic who counts. ... The credit belongs to the man who is actually in the arena, whose face is marred by dust and sweat and blood; who strives valiantly ... who, at the worst, if he fails, at least fails while daring greatly, so that his place shall never be with those cold and timid souls who know neither victory nor defeat."

That was me! I was in the battle! Win or lose, I loved it!

For the first time in my life, success was *on my terms*, and I reached the level of contentment and happiness I always wanted!

I learned my "why" and found my passion.

Now I want to help you find yours. I want to help you get your mojo back. I want to help you live your best life.

How to get the most out of this book:

This book shares the cadence, knowledge, and guidance that I provide to my franchise consulting clients. Everything I do professionally is designed to help you answer a few critical questions:

1.  What is franchising and what are its benefits?

2.  Is franchising right for me?

3.  What is the right franchise for me to maximize my talents and optimize my success?

4.  How do I fund my franchise investment?

This book follows a similar theme. To answer these questions correctly, it is important to have a solid base of understanding of franchising—how it works, its upside and potential pitfalls. In addition, it is crucial to understand and appreciate your unique talents, goals, time commitment, and predilections. They drive, more than anything else, the answers to the critical questions.

Franchising is systems-driven, and to find the right match, I implore you to follow the process laid out in this book, as it provides everything you need to get started and make a truly informed decision.

A seminal part of the process is having a leading franchise consultant help you. Yes, you can do it alone, and some people are very successful with that approach. However, as you begin to explore franchising, your goal should be simple: to optimize your chances of success. A franchise consultant is vital to that.

**Get a Franchise Consultant**

The breadth of concepts, business models, and investment ranges makes it difficult for people to navigate the franchise buying process. This book is a general guide to assist you in the process, but I strongly suggest engaging a franchise consultant as well.

An experienced franchise consultant is an expert in all things franchising and will be able to walk you down a path toward making an informed decision about business ownership. Your consultant should take the time to help you define, clarify, and calibrate your goals. They should be part educator, part matchmaker, part coach, and *100 percent* committed to your success.

Franchise consultants do not sell franchises. Franchisors do that. What I do as a consultant is facilitate a process that enables you to maximize your decision about franchising.

As your trusted adviser, I use my experience, sound professional judgment, and deep market and brand understanding to guide you. I work for you to optimize your franchise opportunities. In doing so, I represent you and provide valuable and unique insights and advice. Franchise consultants are compensated by the franchisor if you join.

If not, the consultant is not compensated. Stated differently, the advice of a consultant is free, but the value is priceless!

If you decide to engage with a franchise consultant, you may see several titles, such as coach, consultant, or broker, as well as modifiers that imply expertise, like "certified" or "senior." Pay little heed to those titles, as they are typically granted by franchise consulting companies for marketing purposes and have little to do with actual expertise.

Here are important traits to seek in a franchise consultant.

First, they must have franchising chops. Look for consultants who have been in franchise consulting for at least a couple of years. From my experience, it takes at least that long to understand all the nuances of franchising, the different sectors, and to hone the necessary skills to coach potential franchisees.

Second, find a consultant who is a thought-leader. Start by reviewing their LinkedIn pages or websites. Are they active? Do they have recommendations? How long have they been doing this? Do they have any published content? Does the consultant have an impressive background?

Next, it is preferable to work with consultants who are or were franchisees. Franchisees possess the added perspective of understanding franchising from first-hand experience. Personally, I could not provide a high level of advice if I were not a franchisee.

Finally, it is important to connect, on a personal level, with the consultant. This is critical because you must feel comfortable sharing personal information, goals, dreams, and fears. Can you be open and honest with this person? Do you trust that they have your best interests in mind? If rapport is lacking, you may be better off finding another consultant.

## Franchising Is Not Right for Everyone

Why do only a small percentage of individuals who explore franchising ultimately decide to invest in one? There are several reasons. For some it becomes clear that franchising is not the right fit. This can be for any number of reasons, including financial, personal, or professional. Still others may not have the right commitment and motivation to be their own bosses. Being in total control of your future is wonderful, but it means *you* are responsible for your paycheck, and that is too much for some people. There is a huge difference between cashing a payroll check and writing one! Others cannot overcome fear. The bottom line is that franchising is not for everyone.

When I first became a franchise consultant, I viewed my role as doing everything I could to find the right fit for clients. Now I see my role as systematically disqualifying people. My goal is to ensure that if you join a franchise, it is the right decision for you on every level—personally, professionally, financially, and lifestyle wise.

Let's get started!

# 1
## MY STORY AND YOURS

*"the stars began to burn*
*through the sheets of clouds,*
*and there was a new voice*
*which you slowly*
*recognized as your own,*
*that kept you company*
*as you strode deeper and deeper*
*into the world,*
*determined to do*
*the only thing you could do—*
*determined to save*
*the only life that you could save."*
—Mary Oliver, *The Journey*

My story is simple. As I rose through the ranks of corporate America, my responsibilities grew, I made more money, and garnered additional recognition. Yet my disaffection and unhappiness grew.

I was unsatisfied and unfulfilled.

I was not present for my family.

I was worn out and tired.

I was frustrated.

I was not enjoying myself.

I was fundamentally unhappy with the career I worked so hard to build.

The hours away from my family, the lack of independence, and the general corporate malaise took a toll. A new job or organization was not going to change that. I was crystal clear that the corporate world could not meet my needs, but I had no alternative path. I was stuck at the intersection of professional success and personal melancholy.

I was raised in New Jersey by wonderful parents. My folks provided everything a parent should to a child: love, confidence, and necessities. They imbued me with a strong sense of self, individuality, and a drive to succeed. I imagine that I can do anything in the world that I want to do.

My parents both worked for large organizations. My father was a research scientist at a pharmaceutical company, and my mother was an educator in a local school system. They worked hard for their salaries, benefits, and pensions. Neither of them owned a business nor, as far as I know, ever thought about opening one. My model was clear: be an employee.

Armed with an undergraduate degree from Penn State University and a law degree from The Ohio State University, I entered the professional world—with a thud. I worked briefly as an attorney before quickly moving into the financial services industry. When I decided to leave the practice of law mere weeks after passing two bar exams, my mom asked, "What am I going to tell my friends?"

That was not my mom's finest moment and is something we laugh about to this day. And it is instructive of three key points.

First, I grew up thinking that you got a job and you kept it, whether or not you were happy or satisfied. Indeed, my dad worked at the same pharmaceutical company from the day he graduated college until the day he retired. My mom worked for the same school system for her entire career. I was taught that exchanging happiness or satisfaction for a paycheck was okay.

The second lesson is that Mark has thick skin. The truth is I do, and that is what helped me rise in the corporate world and eventually earn a high six-figure income. But that was part of the problem. My thick skin masked my unhappiness.

The third lesson is that I have an unshakable confidence. When I left the practice of law, I had no idea what I was going to do with my life. (While it worked out, I do not recommend this course of action!) But I knew it would work out.

After my ever so brief foray into the law, I worked as a financial consultant with Morgan Stanley. I achieved success, was ranked second out of 135 in my training class, and won several awards for performance. While passionate about guiding people to the financial futures that they envisioned, this was not the right long-term fit for me because I did not enjoy following the financial markets.

I quickly transitioned into their management-training program. The focus of the program was training the firm's next generation of financial consultants. I fell in love with training and the idea of helping people achieve their professional goals. I felt a sense of purpose.

As my career progressed, I rose up the corporate ladder, leading training, human resources, and sales teams in financial services and real estate. I made a great living, yet something was missing. Perspective has taught me that when you are climbing a ladder, you focus on the next rung.

Yet regardless of any level of success I achieved, there was always something missing. I wanted freedom and autonomy, but I did not have the guts to venture out on my own. I felt stuck working for others. That was a terribly uncomfortable place for me.

I sought happiness and achievement outside of my primary career. I filled the void by launching my career coaching business, teaching at the university level, and authoring career-oriented articles for newspapers. I needed fulfillment and to stretch and test myself.

I started running trail ultramarathons. I wanted to see what I was made of, how hard I could push myself, and what the limits of my capabilities were. I think, to a large extent, this helped me realize that I was only limited by my imagination.

Running was the antithesis of working for others. It was liberating, enjoyable, and challenging. In contrast to the corporate world and all its restrictions, running provided me with a spiritual freedom and motivated me to find it in my professional life.

Eventually, I was better able to run the business I was working at than the owners of my company, and the results I generated validated that. I approached them and asked to be their partner. It was not about money; I wanted—I needed—to be in control and not work for others.

They agreed to make me a partner, and the negotiations began. They offered me partnership but not the control I coveted. As discussions dragged on, the message was clear: They would not give up control.

After years of trading my personal happiness, family time, and control for a guaranteed income, I needed a change. I told them I was leaving the organization. When the risk of me leaving became real, they made promises I knew they never intended to keep.

Up until this point, I thought I needed the security of

a paycheck to provide for my family. That false belief was replaced by new truths. First, I could generate income with my own business. Second, I was sacrificing more by staying in the corporate world than I was gaining. Finally, while I was providing for my family financially, I was unhappy and not as good a husband, father, son, or friend as I wanted to be.

I wanted to be a better person. I wanted to be a happier person. I wanted to live a more meaningful life. Another corporate job would not help me achieve that.

I went cold turkey and left a high six-figure income to find my path. Friends, families, and colleagues alternated between telling me I was crazy or had a lot of courage. Neither was true. This was the most rational decision I ever made. I believed in myself and wanted more out of life.

And I found it.

Franchising enabled me to overcome the excuses such as fear, inertia, and lack of a compelling idea that kept me from starting my own business on a full-time basis. Investing in a proven business system that provided the marketing, technology, service, and systems that I could not develop on my own made all the difference.

Now I own several successful businesses (all in the franchise space) and have never been happier. The fulfillment I get from being my own boss and helping others is profound. The impact on my life is myriad:

I am a better husband, father, son, and friend.

I am happier in all aspects of my life. *I never knew how unhappy I was until I realized how happy I could be.*

I no longer have a long commute.

I no longer must engage in inane strategy discussions and meetings.

I make quick decisions and execute.

I am proud of what I do.

My schedule is flexible.

I help people.

For me, being my own boss is the best professional decision I ever made. My only regret is I did not transition sooner!

## The Arc of a Career

My path to business ownership is broadly similar to that of many of my clients, although each story is unique.

Most of my clients are doing well professionally and financially when they begin their franchise journey. They are earning great incomes, boast impressive titles, and manage large staffs. However, a key piece is missing or causing frustration in their careers. Some are tired of bosses, others want freedom and work-life balance, or to leave a legacy for their children and grandchildren. Many want out of the nine-to-five grind. Others want an alternative investment vehicle.

All want something different.

The bottom line is that so many of us share similar paths. When you reflect on it, that makes sense. The career arc is exceedingly predictable. Early in our careers it begins with a motivation to learn and express our knowledge, competence, talents, skills, and abilities. We work long hours, play the political game, and take on challenges to achieve. As we climb the corporate ladder, each rung is symbolic proof of our growing talents. We stay fixated on increasing our income and wealth.

The "career ladder" connotes a linear progression, one that is often hard to exit. Over time you can feel like you are in Sisyphean hell. It is both natural and common to question if the career path you chose at 22 is right for you today.

With time, achievement, and a higher net worth, our mindset and priorities evolve, and we seek greater meaning and happiness in our lives. As we strive to self-actualize, changes in our values, motivations, and drives transform us and often lead to dissatisfaction with our careers. Disillusionment and introspection cause us to reconsider how we want to spend the rest of our lives.

Most consider franchise ownership mid-career and there are predictable catalysts for the exploration. Some are internally driven and find their careers unsatisfying and unfulfilling. For others, the motivation is external—losing out on a promotion or being laid off. Regardless of the catalyst, inflection points represent a shift in perspective and motivation, and are predictably inevitable. Even so, most people are not well equipped for this shift. Personally, I was ill-prepared.

For me the inflection point came when my father passed away. I had just turned fifty and was profoundly unhappy at work. As mentioned, my bosses offered me a partnership, but I turned it down. I did not enjoy working for or with them. Their values and motives were very different from mine. My father dying, professional discontent, and recognition of the finite nature of life, were my catalysts for change. I swore never to do anything that did not make me happy.

About that time, I read Bronnie Ware's book *The Top Five Regrets of the Dying*. Ware was a palliative nurse who learned first-hand the remorse individuals experience on their deathbed. The five takeaways are that the dying wished:

1. They possessed the courage to live a life true to their values and not what others expect.

2. They had not worked so hard.

3. They had the courage to express their feelings.

4. They had stayed in touch with their friends.

5. They let themselves be happier.

These regrets were ones I intentionally decided would not be mine! I jumped off the corporate ladder and embraced the broad possibilities that presented themselves. It was a time of personal understanding, exploration, and tremendous energy and power. I was free for the first time in my career to truly pursue what I wanted. And I did not want to work for anyone ever again!

Reassessing what work, and indeed life, means is invigorating but not easy. There is a lot to unpack. If you are leaving a career, you are likely mourning the past as you explore the future. It is natural to grieve what you are leaving behind. After all, that path served you well for a time.

During exploration the world is full of possibilities, as broadly as it was when you began your career. You now have many advantages absent when you launched your career.

First, you probably have more significant resources, financial and otherwise, than when you started off. This creates additional and different options. Second, the breadth and quality of your experience is much deeper. You managed people, ran projects, and accomplished challenging goals. You honed your communication, management, operations, and sales skills. You have a much more refined level of emotional intelligence and can manage the realities of work more effectively. In short, you possess a profoundly stronger skill set than earlier in your career.

Perhaps most importantly, you know yourself much better.

You know your strengths and weaknesses. You can be honest about your abilities, skills, or interests. Career transitioning from a place of experience means you are coming at it from a place of power. Concepts like independence, autonomy, flexibility, and happiness—probably not considered earlier in your career—rise to the fore.

You are a much more complete version of yourself now than when you began your career.

Let's explore business ownership and franchising!

# 2
## FEAR

*"It is not the mountain we conquer, but ourselves."*

—Edmund Hillary, the first person, along with
Tenzing Norgay, to summit Mount Everest

When you consider launching a business, you will be scared. In fact, fear is the number one reason people fail to start their own businesses. Fear is the reason people do not change their lives. Fear, if you let it, can be debilitating.

However, by understanding fear, its manifestations, and using tools to manage it, you can push through the barrier that fear creates and turn your dream of business ownership into a reality.

An important first step is the recognition that the existence of fear is natural. *Everyone* experiences fear, anxiety, and unease when considering large life changes like franchise ownership.

I've coached thousands of people exploring business ownership and all of them are scared. Actually, the ability to manage fear is a rite of passage for business owners. Read these words, take a deep, knowing breath, and recognize that what you are feeling is appropriate and normal.

Let me repeat: EVERYONE EXPERIENCES FEAR.

It is part of the journey to business ownership. When you acknowledge, understand, and accept fear you can conduct your search with the intent and strategy to manage it.

I know the fear of business ownership well. I experienced it, not just through my clients' eyes, but personally. My transition to full-time self-employment was fraught with fear. What I learned from my experience is that fears are wholly linked to emotions and uncertainty. When I committed to learning and gathering facts, data, and information about business ownership, franchising, and specific brands, the opacity that fear created cleared and I was able to make informed decisions. Indeed, I was able to change my life.

**Fear Barrier**

Unmanaged fear causes us to make emotional decisions and persuades smart, successful people to abandon good judgment. A more effective way to make decisions is to focus on facts and use them to lead your emotions. Informed decisions are better than emotionally charged ones.

We like to consider ourselves rational, thoughtful beings

but the reality is often different. Our minds have both a conscious or rational side and a competing subconscious or emotional one. The conscious mind thinks, analyzes, and assesses. It can tell fact from fiction. The subconscious cannot. The subconscious mind is always trying to protect the status quo because change represents risk.

Consider the concept of the fear barrier. The fear barrier is a wall that rises or falls based on the intensity of fear. The greater the fear, the higher the wall. When the fear barrier is low it presents no material obstacle. Eventually, if fear is unchecked, the barrier will continue to rise until eventually it is impassable and halts your progress. Generally, the fear barrier grows the further you are outside your comfort zone.

Let's look at how emotions, fear, and anxiety can cause havoc on your franchise exploration.

You begin franchise exploration full of excitement and energy, focused on the extensive possibilities that business ownership provides. Your catalyst and commitment to investigating franchising is robust, and since exploration is within your comfort zone, your fear barrier is low. When you are in your comfort zone, or not far outside it, your conscious mind holds primacy, and you avoid the subconscious mind's emotional response. A low fear barrier does not generate much resistance and therefore you can easily move forward.

It is when you advance with franchise exploration and extend far from your comfort zone that your subconscious mind's emotional response is triggered, and the fear barrier grows. At this point the rational and emotional minds are competing, and they don't get along well. This is an uncomfortable and difficult space to inhabit. Your emotional side wants you to return to its comfort zone (existing career situation) and stop exploring, while your conscious side wants to become educated and emphasize factual information.

This is the exact moment that you must make a choice: manage your fears or give in to their puerile nature. If you allow your emotions to remain unchecked and unmanaged, you will be so far outside your comfort zone your fear barrier will be extraordinarily high. Panic will set in and stop you in your tracks. You will hit an insurmountable wall. Boom! Your dream of business ownership will be over.

The fear barrier manifests itself in several different ways depending on the degree of fear and the stage of the process. For some candidates, the mere thought of exiting the corporate world, while exciting, provokes so much fear that they catastrophize from the jump. Their self-limiting beliefs overwhelmingly restrict their ability to explore opportunities and they bow out before the process begins.

The next group of candidates manufactures issues so they can rationalize their decisions to stop investigating franchising. By creating challenges that don't exist, franchising becomes the issue, not their fear. For example, they may read a bad review about the franchise online and assume it is a bad business. Or they see a potential competitor and determine the sector is overcrowded. Yet, neither of those conclusions are valid from those singular data points. Unfortunately, fear does not allow them to understand that.

Some candidates simply withdraw from the process with no reference to fact. Comments like "franchising is not for me" or "I am not comfortable" are the taglines. This typically occurs during the latter stages of discovery when decisions about business ownership become real. Again, these decisions are the triumph of fear over facts, and driven by the subconscious.

Finally, some candidates blame external "forces"—almost always a spouse. It is imperative for spouses to both be engaged because franchising is a significant family decision. Most of the time the real obstacle is the candidate's fear.

Regrettably, if you cannot manage your emotions, you will never join a franchise, even when it is in your best interest.

## Life Improves Through Change

Change is hard because of fear and the barriers it presents. Change is also the death of what existed before. When we change, we leave behind many things we value: certainty, comfort, and knowledge. Emotionally we fear replacing them with anxiety, stress, and risk. The deeper you extend into exploration, the more profound the feelings of loss and fear become and at some point, many people succumb to them.

Stasis is the preferred human state and therefore we default to the status quo. Inertia is not just Newton's First Law. It is also the first truth of human behavior: Despite our motivations, goals, and desires, we often don't change, even when we know clearly that it is the sensible approach.

Let me be clear: Fear is not an altogether bad thing. When you manage fear and lever it to heighten your awareness, improve your due diligence, gather facts, and validate brands, it becomes a force multiplier. You just cannot let it rule your life or decisions.

There is a concept in franchising we call trips to the "rodeo". Each time a candidate explores franchising is a trip to the rodeo. Sometimes it takes two or even three trips to the rodeo of franchise exploration to move forward and join a franchise. The reason is twofold. First, often candidates who did not manage their fear effectively when first investigating franchising learn from their mistakes. Second, after staying on the same career path, they realized they were stuck.

I zealously track client metrics. Here are some enlightening ones that speak to the importance of understanding fear and consequences of deference to it. During their first rodeo roughly 20% of my clients join a franchise. Interestingly, that number grows to over 50% when I work with clients who explored franchising in the past!

What accounts for the enormous disparity?

Clients on the first trip to the rodeo do not viscerally understand that nothing changes if they stay on the same course. Those who explored franchising and chose to stay with their existing careers know, on a deep emotional level, that nothing changes.

The funny thing is, very few people who join a franchise ever feel regret. On the other hand, I regularly speak to people who are exploring franchising AGAIN after they previously chose to stay with their careers. To a person, they lament not taking the franchise route earlier. They now realize that by staying in their comfort zones and not managing their fear, they cannot change their lives.

See, the dirty little secret is that sticking with the status quo is generally riskier than change.

Why?

Because absent change, your life will not improve.

Yet despite the perils of staying the same, the aversion to change is powerful. People overvalue what they have vs. what they might have. This bias is called the endowment effect. The endowment effect is a cognitive bias that causes people to place a higher value on something they already possess than the value they would place on the same thing if they did not have it, negatively skewing their assessments. The endowment effect strongly reinforces the status quo.

Why am I telling you this? Because resistance to change is natural, normal, and can be overcome. Franchise ownership is a big change for most people and probably is for you as well. Facing change will create a lot of competing emotions. Emotions such as excitement, fear, hope, and anxiety are natural and to be expected.

## Common Fears

Fear can manifest itself in many ways. Here are a few of the more common types that people experience during franchise exploration.

### Fear of Failure

Most people go through life scared to take risks, since taking a risk increases the chance of failure. Instead, we stay stuck in unrewarding careers or jobs that don't make us happy. Fear of failure can stop us in our tracks and fill our minds with worst-case scenarios. These irrational fears limit our ability to move forward and be the best version of ourselves.

Fear of failure arises because humans tend toward negativity. This is known as availability bias. Bad outcomes appear more significant in our minds than good outcomes. Therefore, you are much more likely to see all the potential negatives in something than you are to see the positives. In other words, it is easier to envision failure than success even though success is the much more likely outcome.

Fear of Change

Most of us live in our comfort zones, doing what we have always done. Inertia keeps us in place. The reality, though, is that the magic happens outside our comfort zones, when we stretch our capabilities. As you proceed deeper into exploration and further from your comfort zone, discomfort grows.

It is important to remind yourself that it is only through change that you will solve your problem. The status quo and being comfortable will not. Magic, growth, and prosperity happen when you venture outside your comfort zone!

Fear of Talent/Experience Gaps

Some people feel trepidation when they explore concepts that are dissimilar to their past experience. On its face this makes sense, since most traditional career paths hire for specific skills (e.g., engineering, operations, finance, or business development) in their specific industry (e.g., oil and gas, construction, medical, or insurance).

However, in franchising, the structure of franchisor business models, systems, and support empower candidates with no specific sector experience to be great franchisees. Franchisors seek transferable skills and teach all the industry specific knowledge needed to flourish. It is important, however, to recognize your true knowledge or skill gaps, and avail yourself of the franchisor's training and support.

Definitional Fear

You are what you think you are. If you believe you are an employee, transitioning into business ownership will be difficult because of your self-limiting views.

Fear of Choosing the Wrong Concept

There are thousands of franchise concepts to choose from. That creates a paradox of choice. In life we want a lot of options, and yet the more choices we have, the harder it is to make decisions, because we think there may be a better one available.

Fear of Opportunity Costs

When you choose a path, you are surrendering others. For example, if you leave behind a corporate career, you may wonder what would have happened if you stayed. Alternatively, if you are considering franchising as an investment, you will weigh it against alternatives such as the stock market or real estate.

## Managing Fear

Generally, when we name a problem, it becomes easier to manage. I ask you for permission to name and discuss your fears. That way we pay homage to a rite of passage and normalize these emotions. The elephant is exposed, and you no longer have to feel like you are in it alone. We all are afraid!

Okay. Now let's discuss how to manage fear.

**Label fear.** Fear is irrational, non-fact-based, worst-case thinking. Focus on what is real. Mark Twain put it well when he said, "I have been through some terrible things in my life, some of which actually happened." Don't limit your life worrying about things that will not happen.

No one likes not being good enough and struggling. However, this is an unlikely outcome of franchise ownership. As in all aspects of life, it is important to take reasonable and calculated chances, and franchising allows you to do that calculus.

**Challenge the status quo.** Commit to completing the franchise exploration process and making a fact-based decision. Nobody changes without the desire to change. There is a catalyst continuum that runs from exploration to action. Said differently, many people possess a catalyst strong enough to explore business ownership, but few have a strong enough commitment to act and launch a business.

If you enter franchise exploration lacking a commitment to follow the process to its conclusion, you are wasting your time. In my experience, the people who succeed, whether they ultimately join a franchise or not, enter the process dispassionately and weigh the pros (reasons driving change) and cons (resistance to change).

**Get the facts.** Do your research and analysis. Franchising makes that particularly easy, because the franchise discovery process with leading brands walks you through every aspect of the business. This allows you to focus on making fact-based decisions, a key component for managing fear. Later, in chapter 10, you will learn about The Perfect Franchise Six-Factor Analysis that supports you in understanding the attributes of each franchise.

**Appreciate how franchising systematically reduces your chance of failure.** Leading franchise brands provide you with proven, repeatable business models, training, support, economies of scale, and so many other resources to encourage your success. Follow the systems and processes and you provide yourself the opportunity to duplicate the results. In franchising, you are in business for yourself but not by yourself. What this means is that the franchise system (franchisor, fellow franchisees, vendors, etc.) will provide ongoing guidance and support.

**Discuss your fears.** When you vocalize your feelings, it helps to both normalize and manage them. Discuss how you are feeling and what you need to effectively manage your emotions. You are not in this alone!

**Seek clarification and support.** The best candidates and franchisees are the ones who ask the most questions. Asking good questions during exploration enables you to swap fears for facts. If you don't understand a concept or are uncomfortable with how you perceive something, ask for clarification. You do not want to decide, or get scared, based on erroneous assumptions.

**Redefine yourself.** Change involves a new self-definition and self-image. Change does not take effective hold without a fundamental redefining. Personally, running a marathon was on my bucket list.

I did not enjoy my first marathon. The training was a chore. I defined myself as merely a guy who ran to achieve a goal. After the race, something strange happened. I missed running. I missed the physical and mental aspects of it. I began to view myself as a runner. It changed everything for me and now I cannot stop running!

Similarly, before I left the corporate world, I redefined myself as a business owner who was currently working for others—an intrapreneur. This self-definition helped me manage my transition out of Corporate America.

Give yourself permission to see yourself as something different than what you have been. Start thinking about business ownership through the eyes of a business owner and not those of an employee.

**Do not overweight the opportunity costs.** Corporate America no longer represents the lifetime contract it once did, and many of its advantages have vanished. In fact, layoffs are commonplace, benefits are being reduced, and workplaces are often toxic.

Why does this matter? Because when you investigate the world of business ownership, it is important to understand that its rewards continue to grow, and the opportunity costs of Corporate America shrink. Simply, you are probably giving up a lot less than you fear!

**Get comfortable being uncomfortable.** Leaving your comfort zone is uncomfortable, and during franchise exploration and launch you will be out of your comfort zone. You cannot become your best self unless you change.

Your comfort zone defines your limitations. Success and greatness come when you grow beyond your comfort zone.

**Believe in yourself.** The more confidence you have in yourself, the less fear will dictate your actions. If you are reading this, you are likely smart, talented, and have a track record of achievement. Why would it suddenly be different when you join a franchise? It will not be. Your level of achievement in a franchise will be high.

**Focus on yourself.** You will hear anecdotes about people becoming fabulously successful or losing everything through franchising. Facts matter; stories do not. Focus on what you can accomplish in a particular franchise that matches your skills, talents, motivations, and goals.

**Harness fear to drive you forward.** Acknowledge your fear and emotions AND continue to move forward. Fear is the opposite of belief, and it is cured with data, information, and evidence. Recognize the uncertainty that exists and act anyway.

**Don't look for a reason to say no.** It is rare to ever be 100% certain about anything in life, so don't use that as an excuse. Few people ever are completely comfortable with any major decision. There will always be variables and unknowns. When you are 80% certain, make a decision. Success in life is predicated on taking reasonable and calculated risks. Look for reasons to say yes!

Again, fear is normal. I don't know any business owners who did not experience fear and anxiety when launching their businesses. What is important is not avoiding fear but rather managing it.

I will leave you with this. It is of supreme importance to handle your emotions and not allow them to dictate business decisions. Sometimes we think that going with our gut is good, but it is a losing proposition that leads to poor, biased, and emotional decisions.

Coaching thousands of people through franchise discovery has taught me that fear and emotional detours always appear. Emotions are unavoidable. And you can choose how to react to them. Acknowledge your fears, and do not let them obfuscate the facts, information, validation, and due diligence you performed.

People who overcome the fear barrier and join franchises seldom regret their decision; people who succumb to fear always do!

# 3
## WHAT IS A FRANCHISE?

*"Systems permit ordinary people to achieve extraordinary results predictably."*

—Michael Gerber, author of *The E-Myth*

Franchising is big business in the United States, with some of the country's most recognizable names leading the way: McDonalds, Meineke, Subway, and Supercuts. Franchising is dominant in industries as diverse as fast food, home services, senior care, and staffing.

A franchise is the right, or license, to market a product or service in a defined territory for a specified length of time. The franchisor grants the right to the franchisee. The franchisee is authorized to use the franchisor's trademarks, marketing system, intellectual property, technology, training, support, and so on, as spelled out in the franchise agreement, in exchange for a franchise fee and ongoing royalties.

Leading franchisors deliver turnkey business models, provide strong and repeatable operating systems, and generate robust revenue streams. They provide the product or service, marketing and sales system, operational infrastructure, technology platform, and world-class initial and ongoing training and support. Importantly, all aspects of the system will be predictable and consistent.

It is precisely the efficient and reliable nature of franchises that makes them desirable and drives their success. In addition, basic business model mistakes and kinks have been worked out of the system. Finally, franchises gain economies of scale because the franchisees band together, pool their resources, experiences, influence, and buying power. That is the power of a great franchise system!

Franchisors provide products and services but, to a large extent, the business model itself is the most important aspect of the business. Following the business model creates expected and recurring results. That is why people flock to franchising as a method to build a business.

The best franchises are ones that you can launch, run, and scale effectively at a lower cost, even with the expenses associated with a franchise, than if you did it on your own.

Franchises come in all shapes and sizes. Investment ranges from $75,000 to millions of dollars. Some are home-based; others require brick-and-mortar locations. Some franchises acquire customers through sales and networking, and others rely on marketing and physical locations to drive business.

There are franchises in every sector of the economy and in

basically every investment range. Once again, to reiterate, the most important aspect of franchising is finding the right fit. Therefore, the key to franchise exploration is finding a brand that matches your personal and professional interests, and financial goals.

The best franchise businesses are systems-based and not people dependent. Yes, you need people, but if the system is good, so are the results. The idea is that people, though a crucial part of a franchise, perform at a higher level because of the systems that define and simplify the tasks. Some brands are so successful at this that they can succeed at a high level even if their product or service is merely good.

For example, you can probably make a better hamburger than McDonalds, but do you want to compete with them? Nope, because they have killer systems. Think about it. One of the most iconic and successful brands in the world is run by a bunch of seventeen-year-old kids flipping burgers and making fries!

That is the power of franchising.

## Franchising Synergies

Franchising enables franchisors to expand their brand without large capital expenditures. In addition, the franchisor relies on franchisees who, as owners, are more vested in outcomes than employees could be.

Franchisees benefit from the ability to execute on a proven business model. Franchisees can avail themselves of the franchisors' support to grow their businesses. Franchisees can focus on executing the business plan instead of creating it from scratch!

At its best, franchising is truly a synergistic relationship that benefits both the franchisor and franchisee. The biggest takeaway is that in franchising, the franchisor and franchisee succeed together.

**Franchise Units**

Franchises are acquired in units. A unit is a defined territory or location in which a franchisee can conduct business. These areas are generally protected. That means no other franchisee of that brand can do business in that area.

Some franchises, such as food, fitness or automotive, are location-based, with a retail location with a certain radius of territory protection. For example, a location can have exclusivity for a five-mile radius. Other franchises such as home service brands do not have retail locations and are territory oriented. Territories are generally defined by the number of people, businesses, homes, and so on, that meet certain pre-defined requirements.

For both territories and locations, leading franchises will focus on building in areas that include an optimal number of ideal customers. Depending on your goals, you may consider single or multiple units as this allows you to grow substantially and scale a business.

## Franchise Fees

There are several fees associated with a franchise and these will vary by brand.

**Franchise fees.** Franchise fees are the price of admission to a franchise. This is the fee the franchisee pays to the franchisor for the right to license use of the brand, its systems, products, or services.

Franchise fees vary, and when purchasing multiple units, franchisors generally reduce each incremental fee. All franchise fees are not created equal. For example, some franchise fees include training or provide a laptop/iPad loaded with company software, whereas others do not include these extras.

It is interesting to note that franchisors usually do not profit on the franchise fee. Indeed, the fee generally barely covers the cost of recruiting, training, and onboarding a franchisee.

**Royalties.** Royalties are the fees paid to franchisors for the ongoing rights to use the business model and support. They are generally paid as a percentage of gross sales, but sometimes can be flat rates. Royalties pay for the franchisor's operating expenses and generate the franchisor's profit. Franchisors use royalties to pay corporate staff and expenses, provide support to franchisees, and generate profit. Royalties vary widely between franchises. The critical aspect of a royalty is not its amount but what you receive for it.

Some brands will have higher royalty costs but provide bells and whistles such as call-center support or client billing. Obviously, these save significant costs and time for a franchisee and are typically well worth the expense. While it is easy to think that a lower royalty percentage is better, that is often incorrect. Do your validation and find out how franchisees feel!

**Ad fund.** Most franchises have a national advertising fee. This is used to create brand recognition, marketing materials, search-engine optimization, and lead generation at the national level.

**Tech Fees.** Finally, franchises charge technology fees. These fees are the passing through of actual costs of program licenses, such as Salesforce or other CRMs, Microsoft Office Suite, and proprietary systems.

A lot of the expenses associated with franchising are ones that you would incur in any business. And in many cases, they are more than offset by financial benefits such as buying products at lower costs because of the franchise volume.

## Franchise Ownership Models

Even the best business systems and support in the world will not help you succeed if you choose the wrong owner-ship model. Ownership model essentially refers to your role in the business. There are three basic franchise ownership mod-els, each with its own set of pros and cons. Each varies sig-nificantly with respect to franchisee role, time commitment, management structure, financials, and scalability. The differ-ent models are:

- Owner-operator

- Semi-absentee owner

- Executive owner

There are stark differences between the models, so it is important for you to decide which model is the best fit for you.

Before discussing ownership models in-depth, it is impor-tant to understand the tradeoff between time, money, and return. All else being equal, the greater a franchisee's time and financial commitment, the better the return and the broader the array of franchise options available. This makes sense because time and investment amount are both drivers and limiters on income potential. Limited assets will act as a cap on your ability to scale and generate greater income. On the other hand, if you lack time, you will need to hire some-one to manage the business, and that will eat into your profits.

Therefore, if you are limited in one aspect (for example, you have little time), you will need more of the other (in this case, money) to improve your returns. There are few viable franchise options when both time and money are extremely limited.

Let's keep the concept of time and money in mind as we look at the different ownership types.

**Owner-Operator:** Owner-operators control all aspects of the business and are directly involved with the delivery of the product or service. Typically, the owner-operator model has a lower initial investment, low overhead, and is normally home-based. The owner-operator is a great option for people who are looking for a career change and want to be responsible for day-to-day operations.

Owner-operators work full-time in the business since they are involved in every aspect of the franchise. Owner-operator businesses have limited scalability because the franchisee is so integral to every aspect of the business. However, franchisees can begin as owner operators, transition into the executive model, and hire employees to scale the business in the future.

**Semi-Absentee:** Semi-absentee ownership is ideal for people who want to stay in their current careers, investors, or retirees who want to add income streams and build equity. Semi-absentee ownership typically requires between ten and twenty hours per week, although the franchisee may spend more time prior to opening, finding real estate, hiring staff, and launching the marketing effort.

Manager-run businesses are best for semi-absentee ownership. Once the manager is trained, the franchisee can begin to spend less time in the business and put systems in place to ensure high performance. The franchisee can focus on strategy, financials, and leading the managers. Semi-absentee owners must have strong management, communications, and people skills. These businesses scale through a combination of investment dollars and strong management.

**Executive:** This is the model for someone who wants minimal time investment or wants to scale aggressively. Executive franchisees generally focus on high-level issues such as financials, marketing strategy, and staffing.

The franchisee hires for all day-to-day functions, including everything from client acquisition to client service. The executive owner can work on the business and focus on expanding into new units. Because the executive model relies on individuals other than the franchisee to perform all the work, it requires significant financial investment on behalf of the franchisee. The flip side is that the executive model is highly scalable and, therefore, has significant earnings potential. For well-capitalized candidates, the executive model is a great option for rapid growth. Hiring the right individuals to run the business is critical to success as an executive owner.

As a franchise consultant, I work with you to understand your ideal ownership model and allow you to transition your business into a less time-intensive one over time. For example, there are ways for owner-operators to scale into a semi-absentee model. Long-term planning is very important for potential franchisees, and I want you to think very intentionally about the future and begin planning for it today!

As you can see, each franchise ownership model has different attributes that do not make sense for everyone. Choose the model that provides you the best opportunity to maximize your success.

## Scalability

In addition to varying levels of ownership involvement, there are also many ways to scale a business. Franchisees can join franchises in different manners. One way is for them to buy a single unit. This provides them the right to one unit, defined as territory or physical location. The second way is for the franchisee to purchase multiple units. This can be done when initially joining the franchise or later, after the franchisee generates success and wants to expand their business footprint.

If you want to build an empire, multi-unit franchising may be the way to go. Multiunit franchisees, as the name implies, own and run more than one location or territory. Multiunit ownership is very common. In fact, multiunit franchisees own over 50 percent of all franchise units.

Franchisors encourage multiunit ownership because it results in improved performance. With multiple units you create a development plan with the franchisor that will allow you to sequentially open your locations. It is important to open over time and not try to launch everywhere at once. Overextending yourself by opening too much too fast is a recipe for failure. Leading franchise brands have models on how to build multiple units both in terms of timeline and team-building protocol.

Success is generally replicable, especially in franchising, and successful operators manage multiple units well and earn additional income in two ways. First, having more units means more revenue and profit potential. Second, they are often able to gain efficiencies and economies of scale, leveraging their infrastructure and staff.

Franchisees learn a lot from their first units and can share management and/or employees between locations. Shared staffing also reduces the risk and stress of employee turnover. Additionally, some franchises provide reductions in royalties above certain breakpoints. These breakpoints are generally based on a franchisee, not a territory or location, so multiunit franchisees are more likely to achieve the discounted status, thus saving royalty payments.

The final benefit of owning multiple units is that franchisees can transition from an owner-operator to a semi-absentee owner. Multiple units provide greater income potential, and that allows for the hiring of a manager to run the business and the owner to reduce their involvement. While possible to do with a single unit, the revenue potential may not make it financially feasible.

# 4
# WHY SHOULD YOU CONSIDER FRANCHISING?

*"Folks are usually about as happy as they make up their minds to be."*

—Abraham Lincoln

Motivation drives success in everything we do in our lives. Without the motivation or drive to accomplish something, you will, absent sheer luck, fall flat on your face. Franchising is no different. To be successful in franchising you must be motivated to be your own boss and put in the necessary time and effort.

Here are some motivators people share when interested in exploring franchising:

"I want more freedom."

"I don't like my boss."

"My job is not secure."

"I want to challenge or prove myself."

"I got passed over for a promotion."

"I want to make money for myself, not for other people."

"I want to be my own boss."

"I want work-life balance."

Those are all good reasons to consider a change, but may not be strong enough motivation to join a franchise. After all, there are other solutions. For example, if you are unhappy with your current job or have been recently laid off, maybe the best option is to find a better job. Deciding to launch a business is not something that should be taken lightly. It needs to be a decision that aligns with your values, interests, and enthusiasms.

People join franchises because business ownership in general, and franchising specifically, provides benefits that they cannot find elsewhere. These are intangibles whose intensity is unique to each individual, with the common goal of aligning the life they live with their values.

When working for other people, we necessarily sacrifice a part of ourselves. We may not have control over our decisions. We may relinquish things that are vital to us, and in doing so we become unhappy and unfulfilled.

I experienced this firsthand. I gave a ton of myself to my organizations but was never fulfilled. Sure, I got a paycheck, but that was not enough for me. I needed more.

I needed to live my values.

## Popular Reasons People Gravitate to Franchising

*Proven Success Model.* Leading franchise systems are turnkey, proven business models with the structure, processes, and resources necessary for success. Franchises should be able to show you that they have successful open units and a methodology to repeat the success. In addition, one of the great things about franchising is that the mistakes have already been made and the systems optimized. Investing in a proven franchise system significantly reduces the risk of failure. Indeed, franchisees succeed at about twice the rate of their non-franchised competitors!

*Client Acquisition.* Franchising provides top-notch brand recognition and state-of-the-art marketing, enabling franchisees to jump-start their efforts to acquire customers and grow thriving businesses. When people think of hamburgers they think of McDonalds and Burger King.

Of course, most franchise brands do not have the same name recognition as those brands, but they make up for it with lead-generation ability. For example, a brand may be a leader in its space, but because of the nature of the business (for example, kitchen remodeling, children's services, senior care, or pet care), it will never be a household name. These brands have world-class marketing that generates client leads.

These marketing efforts are incredibly sophisticated, and the methodology and results are impressive.

*Training Programs.* Franchisors deliver world-class training and development programs that begin prelaunch and continue throughout the life of the business. Programs include classroom and virtual training, business coaching, achiever groups, and conferences.

This allows you to launch the business quickly and efficiently, and provides the ability to scale your business. One-time training events are good, but look for brands that have ongoing support and people you can leverage when you have questions.

*Operational Playbook.* Franchisors systematically help you build and run your business by providing a clear playbook. The playbook lays out all aspects of the business—from client acquisition to product delivery to client service—sharing best practices at every step. This is so important because you want a franchise that will be as turnkey as possible. The more variability in the structure, the more variability there will be in performance.

*People Support.* Franchises have excellent ongoing support; therefore, franchisees are never on their own. Help and expertise in all business areas—including sales, products, marketing, and IT—is never more than a phone call away! In addition, franchisees, while competitive, support each other, exchange ideas, and share best practices.

In franchising, there is always support to help you troubleshoot and solve problems in your business. Some leading brands will provide real-time assistance such as dedicated coaches. Having this level of backing is invaluable. Just remember, it is important to raise your hand and ask for help!

*Technology.* Franchisors invest in cutting-edge technology that supports brand performance. CRMs, inventory, and POS systems are part of the technology suite that franchisors use to empower their franchisees. The technology platform should be a cornerstone of any brand and allow you to optimize each aspect of your business operations.

*The Power of You.* Owners are better than employees. They work for themselves, don't need to play politics, and have skin in the game. Think of all the career successes that you have had up to now. As you put a lifetime of experience to work, the results will follow!

*Franchises Vet Candidates.* Franchisors award franchises to candidates who meet their ideal candidate profile. Effectively screening candidates to match the required skills, strengths, and experiences significantly improves success rates. Filling territories is not enough; they must be filled with the right people. People who do not meet the franchisor's requirements are not awarded franchises.

If the franchisor does not think you are a good candidate for their system, they will not award you a franchise to join.

*Site Selection and Construction Assistance.* When retail locations are required, franchisors perform demographic, traffic, and competitive analysis to identify the ideal location. Once locations are identified, they assist with lease negotiations on behalf of franchisees. This is critical because for brick-and-mortar concepts, real estate is typically the largest expense, especially if a build out is necessary. Some brands have preferred real estate vendors and offer guidance on layout and even furniture. The big takeaway from this should be that leading franchises will support you in myriad ways to ensure your success.

***Economies of Scale.*** Franchise systems' enormous buying power enables them to negotiate significantly lower prices than independent business owners. Superior pricing often offsets fees associated with the franchise.

Buying a proven franchise significantly reduces the risk of failure. No business is guaranteed to succeed, but with the model and support that a franchise provides, franchisees' chances are greatly increased.

# 5
## FRANCHISE SECTORS

*"When asked about what they regret most when they look back on their lives as a whole, people tend to identify failures to act."*

—Barry Schwartz, *The Paradox of Choice*

When most people think of franchising, food concepts come to mind. And that makes sense. About half of all franchise workers are in the quick-service restaurant space, and some of America's most iconic brands reside there. However, some of the best franchise opportunities are in other segments, ones that you may never have even known about.

Franchisors almost never require industry-specific experience. They covet individuals with skills such as business acumen, management, operational, and sales, and can teach you their industry. They are looking for business builders, not industry experts. In fact, most successful franchisees do not have prior experience in the industries they join.

That is important because given the many options in franchising, you do not need to limit your exploration or ultimate choice to something you already know.

Three main segments represent almost all franchises: Retail, home services, and business services. The goal here is to be aware of the breadth and depth of concepts in franchising so you can begin thinking about which ones you are drawn to.

In addition, consider what is driving your interest or disinterest in different sectors. Your perspective provides rich insight into finding the right match.

## Retail Franchises

There are a lot of reasons to consider retail franchises. First, they are generally turnkey and scalable. Retail is great for franchisees who want semi-absentee ownership, and also works well for those that will be involved on a full-time basis. Let's discuss some of the key areas that make up the retail segment of franchises.

**Automotive:** Automotive concepts offer needed services and are turnkey operations. In the auto space it is not important to be an expert in cars. Typically, automotive franchises are involved in repair, maintenance, lube, or aftermarket products.

**Food:** Food franchises are ubiquitous and include household names and emerging brands. Good for semi-absentee or full-time ownership, food concepts are generally available in the quick service (fast-food), coffee, healthy eating, or specialty (bakery, pretzels, etc.) spaces. Food is one of the categories where past work experience is sometimes beneficial.

**Beauty:** This is a sector that includes concepts like hair, nails, eyelashes, etc. Americans care about their appearance, and they are very busy. With people having less and less time in their days, this sector does very well. Licensed employees such as hair stylists and estheticians are often required.

**Health, Wellness & Medical:** As we live longer and with less pain, this area of franchising will continue to grow. Concepts such as massage, med-spas, weight-loss, and pain management help us to feel good. These concepts often require employees to have a higher skill level and sometimes involve medical oversight.

**Fitness:** There are a lot of great opportunities in the boutique fitness area. This space is often class-driven and has a high retention and commitment level. Think boot camp, cycling, yoga, and specialty fitness such as stretching. These are great for semi-absentee and multiple franchise ownership.

## Home Services

Home services are a strong area for franchising, and one that most people do not initially consider. Home services is a broad category that includes any product or service for a house or delivered in a house. With the DIY baby-boomer generation aging and staying in their homes longer and younger generations less interested in doing projects, this category will see continued growth. This sector delivers strong lead generation, has diffuse, mom and pop competition, and solid unit economics. Certain brands within this group provide call centers, appointment setting, and even basic sales. Some of the categories that make up home services include:

**Remodeling and Design:** Consider all the projects that can be done in a house and there is probably a leading franchise brand dominating that market. Kitchen and bathroom remodeling, organizational solutions, flooring, garage solutions, and painting are just a few of the concepts in this area. Powerful lead generation and systems support this group of brands.

**Maintenance:** Maintenance is a needed service. So, whether it is a plumbing, landscaping, junk removal, roofing, or electrical contracting franchise, it is generally recession-proof and does not require you to have the expertise—you hire for it!

**Cleaning:** Once a luxury, residential cleaning is now a necessity and that is driving growth. This is a strong recurring revenue business with a high client retention rate and strong franchisor support. Again, you are not doing the cleaning. You are running a cleaning business!

**Restoration:** The ultimate recession proof industry,

restoration focuses on remediation of water, fire, smoke, and mold damage. It is a highly fragmented business full of opportunity since issues such as fires or burst pipes occur regularly. Plus, most of the remediation is paid by insurance.

**Real Estate:** This is a broad category that includes property management, wholesaling of homes, home inspection, and staging services. This is a great area for both people with experience in real estate and people with relationships with realtors.

**Senior Care:** With the population aging and seniors choosing more than ever to stay in their homes, senior care is a booming business sector. There are three main aspects of senior care: companion care, skilled care, and placement assistance. All of these areas can expect high growth for the foreseeable future.

**Child Related:** Education, sports, and entertainment make up the children's sector. People spend money freely on their kids, so this is a space with unlimited potential. Some of the concepts have brick and mortar locations, but a number are home based.

**Pet Care:** Americans love their pets, and it shows with opportunities such as grooming, daycare, and traditional retail stores. This is an area for franchisees who have an affinity for pets, but that is not required. Both retail and home based businesses are available in the pet space.

## Business to Business

Business to business is a solid area because services such as training, coaching, staffing, printing, marketing, IT, and financial are always coveted. This is an area that requires more proactive outreach and works well for people who enjoy sales, have a strong white-collar background, and are comfortable with a longer sales cycle.

**Coaching and Training:** These concepts focus on the development and improvement of employees—something all types of companies need. By driving performance, coaching and training franchises are in high demand!

**Technology:** Small and mid-sized companies outsource their IT services. Because it is not economical for them to hire and staff an IT department, this is an area of strong opportunity.

**Staffing:** Franchise staffing firms are major players in the market for employers needing permanent and temporary personnel.

**Advertising and Marketing:** Sign companies, print shops, and marketing firms benefit significantly from franchise expertise and purchasing power, making this a category where franchise concepts perform well.

**Financial:** This is another area where small and mid-sized organizations often lack the bandwidth or expertise and therefore outsource. Concepts include cost reduction, bookkeeping, and even outsourced CFO's!

While 90%-95% of franchise concepts are included in the categories discussed, there are some specialty areas such as CBD, laundromats, and others that do not fit neatly into a segment.

Remember that the franchisor is not looking to you to be the expert in that field. You are almost never providing the service, instead relying on people you hire or the franchisor for that. Find businesses that play to your business acumen and individual strengths.

Interestingly, affinity for an area can often lead to reduced income.

Why?

Because liking and being interested in a concept area does not mean it is the right fit. Challenge your comfort zone. We all develop preconceived notions, and a benefit of franchise exploration is that you can confirm or invalidate your perspective about brands or industries. Similar to judging a book by its cover, it is hard to understand industries and concepts from the outside.

# 6
# THE FRANCHISE EXPLORATION PROCESS

*"Chance favors the prepared mind."*

—Louis Pasteur

There are several ways to find a franchise. You can:

- Conduct a Google search.

- Go to franchise portals.

- Choose from a franchise ranking list.

- Ask your friends and family if they know anyone who owns a franchise.

- Throw darts at a list of franchises.

**Or you can optimize your search.**

There is a clear way to elevate your franchise exploration and discovery, and I will lay it out for you. This system has guided thousands of people to successful business ownership through franchising. In my experience, the closer someone adheres to the model, the better the outcome.

The approach will transform unknowns, fears, and uncertainties into facts, data, and knowledge so you can make an informed decision. Whether or not you ultimately join a franchise, it is my goal that you will make a rational, fact-based decision.

There are three critical steps to finding the right franchise:

1. *Understanding and Introspection.* During this foundational step you will learn about the basics of franchising and clarify your motivations. This stage requires a high level of introspection, as you will consider questions such as:

    • Why do you want to own a business? (Addresses pain and motivation)

    • Do you want to enter a business on a full-time basis, or would you prefer to keep your current job and build something on the side? (Time commitment defines business type)

    • What are you good at professionally? (Skills and strengths define ideal fit)

    • What do you struggle with in the workplace? (Weaknesses are areas to avoid)

    • What are your fears about business ownership and franchising? (Yes, you have them!)

- What is your net worth, credit score, and liquidity? (The number one reason businesses fail is because of lack of financial wherewithal)

These questions drive self-examination, increase understanding, and elicit anything germane to identifying, launching, and managing a business successfully. I use a combination of written questionnaires and conversations to gather this information.

The other aspect of the understanding stage is education on the basics of franchising. That is one of the reasons I wrote this book. I want you to make informed decisions and have a context for due diligence. Knowledge includes different aspects of franchising, including sectors, success factors, funding options, and expectations.

2. *Business Model and Matching.* During this stage, the information is assimilated into a personalized franchise business model. Essentially, this will be the blueprint for your perfect franchise brand and serve to guide the process forward. Fundamental is to identify the critical business features you seek.

Next, the business model is juxtaposed to leading franchise brands. This step is part science, part art, and heavily research-based. When I perform it for you, I rely on my knowledge of you and franchise brands. During matching I will identify a handful of brands that match your business model and will have resonance in their location. Essentially, these are the brands that you would choose for yourself!

3. *Due Diligence and Discovery.* This is when you learn all aspects of the individual franchises. During this step, you speak regularly with the franchisor, review documents, and connect with franchisees. You will learn everything you need to make an informed decision.

   I communicate regularly with you during due diligence, debriefing and sharing insights. Due diligence is a methodical, thoughtful, and efficient approach to exploring franchise ownership. I will also introduce you to the best franchise professionals, folks who specialize in franchise financing, franchise attorneys, insurance professionals, and accountants.

There is actually a fourth step in the process—hire a top franchise consultant to guide you. That this is a gratuitous plug does not make it any less true. The guidance of a leading consultant is invaluable and free. Consultants are paid by the brands, not the franchisee, so if you join so there is no extra cost to you!

## Keep In Mind

Be open-minded. Be open to different industries and concepts, even ones you never considered before. For example, few people grow up excited to enter the fields of window coverings, cost reduction, or sign manufacturing, but those are incredibly successful franchise sectors.

Obviously, the business and sector play roles in the decision. However, to maximize your success, it is essential to find a business that matches your style and talents.

**Go at a comfortable pace.** Explore franchising from a position of strength. As you enter the process, there is no obligation or commitment to join. Just follow the process and be true to who you are and your vision of your life. So, take your time; go at your pace. The franchise exploration journey typically takes sixty to ninety days. If finding the right fit takes more time for you, that is okay.

**Decide.** Don't be afraid or hesitant to make a decision once you have all the facts. If additional information is needed, create a plan to get it. Once you complete your due diligence and have all necessary information there will still be a leap of faith, and some degree of fear. At this point procrastination becomes a bad word. You will never, ever be 100% certain. If you are 80% confident, you are ready to decide.

**Be Honest.** It is important that you are introspective and authentic with yourself. If the inputs are bad or inaccurate, you will get suboptimal results. Take your time and be thoughtful, intentional, and open in what you share with your consultant. Bad information may generate less than ideal results.

**Prepare.** This is where consultants add tremendous value. They will provide resources and tools, help you analyze information, and empower you to put your best foot forward.

Stick to the process and you will make a logical decision. Your unknowns and fears will be traded for information, financial models, and validation.

## How the Process Ends

A high percentage of people who conduct due diligence eventually join a franchise. But not everyone does, and that is okay. Decisions about careers, business ownership, and indeed life are very personal, and the goal is simply to enable you to make non-emotional decisions.

There are three common outcomes to completing the franchise exploration process.

1. You find a franchise that resonates with you and join. Happy ever after.

2. You are very interested in franchising and want to recalibrate and explore different brands. We circle back and find the right concept.

3. You decide that franchising is not the right path at this point in your life.

There is one additional, suboptimal outcome: some

candidates, though not you, do not follow the process and fail to make an informed decision. Fear drives their decisions, confirms their preconceived notions, and they bow out of the process prior to gaining the facts. To paraphrase the great physicist Edward Teller, knowledge is what we strive for, but relying on false knowledge is the biggest problem people create in their lives.

Let's dig deeper into each step.

# 7
## KNOW THYSELF

*"The unexamined life is not worth living."*

—Socrates

The Federal Trade Commission (FTC) restricts any earning claims from franchisors or franchise consultants outside item 19 of the Franchise Disclosure Document (FDD—more on this in chapter 11). This is an awesome rule because it focuses you on what is most important to your success: a franchise that meets your personal, professional, lifestyle, and financial goals.

Yet this is at odds with the first question you want to ask: "how much money can I make?" Of course, you want to know the earning potential; after all, making money is a major reason you are considering joining a franchise in the first place!

However, there is a little secret in franchising that most candidates don't know.

It is irrelevant what *other* franchisees earn. All that matters is what *you* can make. There is no nexus between the income of others and your performance. There is variability in franchisee success in every leading franchise, and it is due almost entirely to the fit or the franchisee. Stated differently, some franchisees perform well, and others struggle. Remember, this is occurring in franchises that provide the same business models, territory demographics, and support to all their franchisees. Therefore, the variation is not system based.

Indeed, not all franchisees are created equal, and it is their differences that account for the variabilities in performance. When a franchisee's skills, strengths, goals, and commitment match those of a franchise, they can perform well; when they do not, it will be a struggle. The most important part of finding a franchise is defining your skills, abilities, and goals and matching them to franchise brands.

Joining a franchise can be one of the great positive inflection points in your life. You can take control of your destiny, change the course of your career, and build income and wealth. Sounds good, right? There is a catch.

Inflection points can go well, but they can also go poorly.

Again, franchising success comes down to fit. It really is that simple! Let's discuss a question that is often raised: "Is there a 'right' type of personality for franchising?"

The answer is a resounding no! All personality types can succeed as franchisees. However, there is a right type of personality and skill set for most individual franchise concepts. Finding the right fit is so important, and that is why the emphasis is on matching your demeanor, personality, and skills to a brand.

Personality and communication style matters in a franchise. Some brands and systems look for franchisees who are very assertive salespeople, and others look for good business managers. Some seek detail-oriented candidates, and others want big-picture thinkers. For every personality style there are associated franchise opportunities.

At this stage, focus on franchise concepts that maximize your innate skills and talents. By playing to your strengths, you optimize your chances and magnitude of success!

**Fit and Match**

Okay, you want to be in business for yourself and have the financial ability to make it happen. You have a good understanding of franchising and how it works. And you believe it is a great vehicle for you. Congratulations!

Now is the time to identify what you are looking for in a franchise. It is time for introspection. Now zero in on your skills, wants, interests, and preferences.

The following questions will help you pinpoint and prioritize the factors that are important in franchise ownership. Before looking at my interpretation and feedback on each question, take thirty to forty-five minutes to answer the questions. Write down your answers so they are memorialized, and you can refer to them in the future.

*What does successful business ownership look like for you five years from now?*

The purpose of this question is to get you thinking on a high level, so it is deliberately open-ended. Do you prioritize the financial, lifestyle or professional aspects? Do you want the pride that comes with accomplishment, or are you more interested in the flexibility a successful business can provide? Is your focus on control and not having a long commute or a difficult boss? Thoughts that we have on top of the mind are usually important, therefore take note of what comes immediately to mind. This question helps you determine what you want your business and life to look like.

*What is your professional superpower?*

Your superpower is the skill you are better at than anyone else. This simple question can provide a lot of direction in your search for a franchise. I hear answers across the spectrum. Frequent superpowers include communications, management, leadership, sales/business development, operations, financials, accounting, customer service, time management, project management, and team building.

This is a powerful question because that delivers a lot of focus. For example, if you are good at and like sales, you should focus on franchises where sales or business development is required. If you are strong at managing others or building teams, identify franchises that involve building teams. While playing to your strengths sounds intuitive on paper, it is not always in practice. It is easy to get distracted by a hot or cool concept and lose sight of the fact that it is not the right match for you. If needed, I will redirect you to stay focused on the concepts that make the most sense for your skill set!

*What is your kryptonite?*

This is a companion to the superpower question and pays homage to the Superman franchise (not one you can join!). It helps you identify skill deficiencies or areas that, even if you are competent, are of no interest to you. We all have weaknesses, but our successes are predicated on avoiding them.

Let's unpack this. First, as the owner of any business, you will need to do things that you may not love. That comes with being the boss. What is important, however, is that you do not join a franchise where the core of the franchisee's role is something you abhor. That would set you up for disappointment or unhappiness.

About a year ago I spoke to a candidate who joined a B2B franchise that required a lot of sales skills. He stated that he found the brand on his own without the use of a consultant. On our initial call he told me that he wanted to add another brand to his portfolio. I asked him the kryptonite question, and he responded that his weakness was sales. Knowing that the concept required a lot of sales, I asked him how he decided to join the B2B brand. His voice dropped and he said that he thought the product was cool and therefore he did not focus on the mismatch. The poor alignment between his skills and the brand cost him money and a lot of lost sleep!

*Are you good at building and managing teams?*

This is really two questions wrapped in one. Building teams addresses finding, interviewing, and training others, while managing is the result of that effort. People with experience managing others and who like doing it can succeed in franchises where they are able to build teams to service customers. On the other hand, if you lack the skills or motivation to manage others, look for owner operator concepts.

It is important to really think this through. I had a candidate who ran a mid-sized construction company. He managed a team of over a hundred. When I asked him what he was looking for in a franchise, he said, "not to manage anyone." On further discussion, he was simply burned out from the responsibility of managing scores of people and wanted a small business with less than a handful of employees. The universal truth is that being good at something does not mean you like it or that you should do it.

*What is your ability and desire to sell?*

This is a question that trips up a lot of people. There are three aspects of sales, and it is important to understand them and match with the franchisor's expectations.

First is the ability to build a sales pipeline. This typically requires a lot of outreach, such as cold-calling or networking. Unfortunately, a lot of franchisees mismatch on this attribute and struggle or fail. When you speak to franchisees during validation, this is an important question to ask because if you get this wrong, failure is almost guaranteed.

The second aspect of sales is consultative selling. Consultative selling occurs when you are one-on-one with a client, understand their needs and goals, and offer solutions. This requires strong communication skills, asking good questions, and active listening. More people are comfortable with this aspect than with filling the pipeline.

The last aspect of sales is relationship management. After a client begins working with you, the communications will be ongoing to ensure their expectations are exceeded. Most people are comfortable with this aspect of sales.

Here is a simple continuum of the ways to develop a sales pipeline. Think about which methods you are most comfortable with and focus your search on franchises that require that level of sales drive or less.

*Cold calling:* This requires the highest sales drive. Cold calling, as the name implies, means that you are calling on individuals or businesses that you have no prior relationship with. Essentially you are hunting for customers. For most people, the rejection of cold calling makes it the most difficult aspect of sales. However, if cold calling is a strength, the earning potential is nearly unlimited.

*Networking:* Like cold-calling, networking involves actively soliciting business from others, but in this case, from people you know or through groups with whom you have relationships. Examples of networking include attending functions such as Chamber of Commerce or industry group events, booths at conferences or home shows, social media like LinkedIn, or reaching out to contacts you already know. Networking is easier than cold calling but includes a significant commitment on your part.

*Following up on incoming inquiries:* Many franchisor models drive business to the franchisees. Customers are generated from marketing campaigns, social media, pay per click (PPC), and other methods. These potential customers expressed an interest in your service. In these situations, you will need to speak to the person and schedule an appointment, perhaps in their house or business, and consult with them about your product or service. Some franchisors even have call centers that schedule the appointments for you. In this situation you are still selling but do not need to find the customers; instead, you simply need to deliver your pitch and compete for, and win, their business.

*Do you need to be passionate about a specific business or passionate about being in business for yourself?*

Many clients believe they need to be deeply attracted to a concept or sector. I understand and appreciate this perspective, but it can lead to bad decisions. In the majority of franchises, the franchisee will not be delivering the product or service. Instead, a team of employees or contractors will be doing the work and the franchisee will be running the business.

Find brands where your passion is for the role you, the franchisee, will play in the brand. In other words, within franchise sectors, owners typically perform similar roles. Most home services brands, for example, require the franchisee to manage the business (marketing, financials, administrative), consult with customers, and hire the team. And, while the product can be as varied as painting, insulation, kitchen remodeling, or pest control, the role of the franchisee is comparable.

Find your motivation for being your own boss. That includes being passionate about:

- Succeeding

- Executing

- Growing a business

- Not answering to anyone

- Making your own schedule

- Working your tail off for you

- Reaping the rewards of your effort

*Does your family support you in joining a franchise?*

Family support, typically spousal, is critical. I get very excited when spouses join a client call without prompting. Starting a business is a family affair. Because of this, buy-in from loved ones is important. Clients must include spouses or partners in exploration. Sometimes family members will also be joining the business. In most situations, spousal buy-in is a critical support mechanism for clients.

I remember distinctly one of my clients telling me his wife supported him and would approve of any franchise he chose to join. Turned out he was wrong. When it was time to sign the franchise agreement, she pushed back. Once my client's wife performed her own discovery, they joined the franchise. And my client learned a lesson.

My wife always supports my business endeavors and wants me to be happy. While 'happy husband, happy life' is not an aphorism, it probably should be! She knew that if I continued in the corporate world, I never would be my best. Having my wife's support has been crucial to my success and to our relationship.

*How would you rank the following in order of importance when choosing a franchise?*

1.  Better work-life balance

2.  Current income

3.  Desire to build equity

4.  Freedom

Franchising can provide a lot of benefits, and understanding your motivations is important. This simple ranking question helps you better appreciate what you are trying to accomplish through business ownership.

*What is your ideal location for a franchise?*

Seems like an easy question, and generally it is. If you are committed to living in the same area indefinitely, there is no reason to consider any other location. Franchise ownership shortens your commute and allows you to leverage preexisting relationships and networks.

However, occasionally there are extenuating circumstances, such as the possibility of moving to another state. If there is a high likelihood of moving a significant distance, it may make sense to put off the search until you make a decision. It is important to be near your business, so you really need to think hard about where you want to launch, or it can turn into a headache as you are planning your life!

*Do you want employees, and if so, how many, and what type?*

The question of employees looms large because employees allow you to scale. But you also need to be capable of, and committed to, managing others. There are a plethora of options. You can go solo, have a small team, or build a large one. You can choose a business with white collar, retail, skilled contractors, caregivers, or craftsmen. You can choose a business with employees or independent contractors.

Let's look at the variables. The first decision is whether you want employees at all. During most of my corporate career, I managed scores of employees and enjoyed it. When you manage other people, you spend a lot of time developing, training, and helping them manage challenges. I found this rewarding at the time; however, when I left the corporate world, I had no interest in managing people. I made the conscious decision to go into business alone with the idea that if anything, I would hire one or two people to support me. Therefore, I chose a business I could run by myself. It was the right decision for me, but as with anything, there are plusses and minuses.

Working by yourself:

Pros

- You control everything.

- No time is spent managing or developing others.

- You are wholly responsible for the business's success or failure.

Negatives

- You make no money when you don't work.

- It is not scalable.

Teams:

Pros

- The business is scalable by hiring more people.

- You can hire for things you don't want to do.

- The business makes money even when you are not actively involved.

Negatives

- It is harder to control outcomes, quality, service, and so on.

- You assume a greater financial burden.

- There is a time commitment to training and developing your employees.

*Do you prefer a home-based business or a physical location?*

When I launched my business, I wanted flexibility and to work from home. I was fortunate to have a room in my home that turned into a comfortable and productive office space.

Advantages of working from home:

- There are fewer expenses.

- Productivity can increase.

- There is more work and family flexibility.

- A better work-life balance can be created.

- There are no rent expenses.

- There is no commute.

- Family can get involved.

There are potential tax benefits if your space passes the "exclusive use" test, and you can show it is your principal place of business and is used regularly and exclusively. If you work off your kitchen table and use that area for family dinners and other activities, the IRS won't let you take a deduction on it. Always consult a tax advisor.

Disadvantages of working from home:

- You never leave the "office," and that can impact work-life balance

- Distractions—kids, dogs, and so on—must be dealt with.

- Your home is not set up for work.

- There are no peers to physically interact with.

- Did I say dogs? They visit a lot!

*Do you prefer to work with business or consumer customers?*

This is an important decision because stylistically, the sales cycles and approaches are different. Business to business sales is going to be more structured, have a longer sales cycle, and is great for people who are comfortable in a formal corporate setting.

Selling to consumers is generally more casual, with most sales presentations occurring at the customer's kitchen table.

*Can you follow a system?*

Following a game plan is central to franchising. It is what you are paying for, and why leading franchise systems flourish. If you cannot follow directions, then stop reading this book! The people who succeed in franchising are the ones who follow the plan and avail themselves of the franchisor's resources. The best franchisees value the franchisor's expertise and ask the most questions.

*Do you prefer established or emerging brands?*

Established brands are ones that have been around for a while and often have lots of existing locations. These brands typically provide more structure and less autonomy than emerging brands. Emerging brands offer more access to the leadership team and better territory availability. This difference speaks to the type of culture you want to associate with when you join a franchise.

*On a scale of 1 to 10, how much do you want to own your own business?*

With 10 being the highest, this is a simple question. In my experience, anyone who rates their desire at less than a 7 does not have enough entrepreneurial drive to launch a franchise. While it is easy for clients to provide a number, I always follow up with "Why?" That is not as easy to answer. A lot of people want to be their own bosses but are unable to articulate why and that says a lot.

## Finding Your Why

I speak with scores of potential franchisees each month, and they express a variety of reasons for why they want to explore franchising. Here are the primary ones:

- Control over their life

- Be their own boss

- Don't want to work for others

- Create wealth

- Spend too much time at work

- Current income

- Diversification (some view franchising as a different asset class)

- Create a family legacy

- Positive impact on others

- Get a better return than other investments

Now here is where it gets interesting. Reasons are not the driver behind making big decisions. When I work with you, I really try to understand your "whys". A "why" is a clear and cogent motivation. Identifying your "why" is not easy, but once you know it, you can move forward with purpose, confidence, and determination.

Your "why" is the overarching, unifying idea that informs your decisions. It's the way you engage life and draw on your personal talents and abilities. It is how you self-actualize and live your best life.

Let me share with you my "whys" and how they relate to my career decisions. First let me say that it took a lot of time and soul searching to understand my "whys". When I was on the corporate hamster wheel, I lacked the understanding and congruence I do now, and it has made a huge difference in my life. These are the underpinnings of every decision I make.

My personal "whys" are:

1. I want to provide for my family. That means I need to make a good living and be present in their lives. The reality is I can do this with some jobs or a variety of

businesses. So, this is not the real differentiator of my career choice.

2. I want to help others achieve their goals. be happy, and to feel as excited as I am about their work. I want to help people self-actualize. Once again, I can do this in different jobs or businesses, so this is not dispositive of my career choice.

3. I covet challenges. I conquered the corporate world. And that is why I started running. I wanted to understand my capabilities. I started my first business and every subsequent business for the same reason. I want to push my limits, and franchising allows me to do that. Still, I can find challenges in the corporate world or through multiple businesses. Again, this does not drive my career decision.

4. I need freedom and autonomy. This is pathological for me. I have a fiercely independent streak that borders on obsession. I do not want anyone to control me or my decisions. No workplace would ever be able to afford me the freedom I covet; I need to own my own business. This "why" is a huge part of me that I subjugated for years in the corporate realm and the reason I bumped heads with my bosses. In addition, I do not want geographic restrictions. My compulsion for freedom, autonomy, and independence is my big career driver, and one that only business ownership

could provide. So, this is where I started my search and I looked at owner-operator models that fit my other "whys".

Once I possessed this clarity I needed to decide if I was going to keep sacrificing my values or if I had the courage to make a change and be congruent. Ultimately, by aligning my "whys" and my career, I have achieved a level of personal and professional success that was beyond my reach in the past.

Finding your "why" or purpose is directly correlated to your ability to ask, and answer, good questions.

What are the right questions to find your "why?" Here you go! These will help you begin to bubble up the "whys" in your life so you can align them with your vocation. Alignment is a power multiplier for happiness and success.

- Why do you get up in the morning?

- What passions do you pursue in your free time?

- What are the roles, responsibilities, and things that you gravitate to?

- What are the tasks and responsibilities you avoid or dislike in your career?

These questions provide a good start in performing the introspection and self-dialogue that is required to calibrate the right franchise fit. You have a lot to think about.

# 8
## MATCHING

*"Sometimes I look at you and wonder how I got so damn lucky!"*

—Mark Schnurman, speaking to his wife.

You are moving through the process and have completed the hard work of introspection by clarifying your goals, expectations, and strengths, and have a solid foundation in franchising and some of the key segments. Now it's time to identify franchises that are potentially good matches. The goal is to prioritize your preferences and strengths and measure them against leading brands, finding the ones that best match you and your goals.

As a franchise consultant, I will create a detailed, personalized franchise business model for you. The model is based on the rich information you share with me. This model will be used to match you to leading franchise brands.

## Elements of Matching

Once your franchise business model is created, compare it to leading brands to identify a fit. This is essentially using a Turing system. Input (your ideal business model) X Function (matching process) = Output (recommended brands).

During matching, research brands that make sense from both a personal and location standpoint. Things like climate, demographics, and population density are important considerations.

Matching occurs across many different aspects of business. While the specific order of evaluation and matching is predicated on the intensity of the factors for individual clients, the following are the ones that resonate across the board.

**Investment.** Simply, it makes no sense to perform due diligence on concepts you cannot afford. Don't just focus on the cost of entry but also the ongoing cost of running a business and the timeline for cash flow break even.

**Ownership model.** Only look at the ownership model or models that you are interested in. A word of caution here. A lot of franchises claim they can be managed on a semi-absentee basis, and while that is true, most cannot be launched that way.

**Lead generation.** Decide on whether or not you want to build your client pipeline through your efforts or if you prefer brand lead generation. Brands with powerful lead generation engines may be able to launch quickly.

**Time commitment and flexibility.** Many people explore franchising to create work-life balance, making this a critical factor to consider.

**Scalability.** How big do you want to build your business? Almost any franchise will provide the ability to invest in multiple units so you can scale. That then ties back to a few other considerations, such as how many employees and the investment range, because multiple units will have more employees and an additional cost.

**Business or consumer customers.** Many people have a strong preference for one type vs. the other.

**Size of staff.** How many people do you want in your business? For example, if you only want a handful, it narrows the search for exact available brands.

## Benefits of Having a Consultant

Matching is an area where a consultant can add a lot of value.

A consultant has the knowledge, experience, and tools that allow for the consideration of many more brands than you can research on your own. I work with a portfolio of hundreds of franchises—the largest group of leading brands in the industry. I have serious tools that permit me to quickly sift through the brands for match, location availability, and a variety of other factors. If you conduct the search on your own, you will be very limited in the brands you can easily research and assess.

In addition to my knowledge of the brands, I am constantly learning more about them. I am frequently on educational calls. I hear feedback from clients validating with them, and gain feedback from industry colleagues.

I use all of these insights during the matching stage AND share insights with you along the way. This is the power of a good franchise consultant.

Finally, I want to share my innate biases, so all know my perspective in identifying brands.

First, I only look at brands in sectors that will be around for a long time. If a concept is a fad there is a strong chance that franchisees will struggle when consumer tastes change.

Second, I only recommend brands that are Amazon proof. There is no reason to enter a business that technology or online shopping can easily impact. Even though the business may do well, there is too much risk.

Third, I seek the simplest brand models in a sector. All else being equal, the less moving parts a concept has, the easier it is to launch, grow, and scale. There is no need to complicate a business.

Fourth, I look for brands that can launch more quickly than their peers. Some factors that lead to a quick launch are strong franchisor lead generation, a short sales cycle, and a more transactional nature of the business.

Finally, I seek brands that have strong ROI relative to their peers. This generally means that between two similar brands, I will recommend the brand that has the lowest cost of entry because, assuming the same income, investment amount will drive ROI. For example, assume there are two home service brands in which the franchisee will perform similar roles and have similar income expectations. Brand A is a simple model with very little equipment and a low employee count. Brand B requires a lot of equipment, trucks, and employees. In this scenario, Brand A is the better investment and the one I will recommend.

## Common Mistakes in Franchise Matching

A mentor of mine once said that affluent people want to own restaurants and that the truly wealthy gravitate to hotels. At the time I did not know what to do with the comment.

What he meant was that restaurants and hotels are status symbols, and the images of them, not the economic or operational realities, were the primary decision points. Yet, the perceived prestige or "coolness" of an opportunity is the wrong decision point. Consider only franchises that play to your strengths and talents.

The optimal approach to finding the right franchise is by

being open-minded and matching your franchise goals, skills, interests, and motivations with the models of the leading franchise brands. Let me share some tendencies people have that get in the way of a successful match.

- As noted, some candidates fall in love with a concept regardless of whether they have the skills, time, or finances to make it successful. This often happens with retail locations such as gyms, restaurants, or spas.

- Candidates often overestimate their abilities. While your skill set is not fixed, it makes no sense to join a franchise that requires managing twenty people if you have no management skills. Franchises will teach you about their concept and sector, but heavy management or sales training is not generally on the agenda.

- Lack of goal clarity or motivation make it difficult to hit the mark; inaccurate inputs lead to bad outputs.

- Other candidates do a poor job of validation and do not understand the true expectations of a franchisee.

- Candidates may not understand the nuances of each different brand.

The next step is for you to begin speaking with the franchisor. This is the beginning of brand due diligence.

## Speaking to Brands

Sometimes clients feel the urge to conduct research prior to speaking with the brands. This is a fear-based response, a suboptimal practice, and a waste of time. Here's why. First, success in franchising stems from following a proven system. The franchise exploration model I use has successfully placed thousands. And the best outcomes come to those who adhere to the process. When people deviate, their success rate is much lower. Also, research at this stage produces very limited useful information. The only way to truly learn about the models—value propositions, earnings potential, etc.—is by speaking with franchisors and validating with franchisees. Finally, the top franchises are in demand and units sell quickly. Any delay in the search could mean losing a great opportunity.

Keep in mind that speaking with the franchisors does not commit you to anything more than a couple of calls. It is simply how you educate yourself about the brands.

# 9
## RISK

*God does not play dice with the universe.*

—Albert Einstein

Risk is a profound blind spot for most people. Few of us possess the innate knowledge or ability to define, recognize, analyze, and mitigate risk. This is especially true in franchising. Here are some reasons for this. First, people often conflate fear and risk. They are two fundamentally different concepts. Second, most do not understand the components that drive risk. Finally, people generally extrapolate their abilities from one arena to another and while the majority of people possess no business risk mitigation experience they think they do.

## How to Measure Franchise Risk

When defining franchise risk, clients almost always discuss losing their money and failure as the primary risks. Since risk is traditionally thought of as the likelihood of loss or injury this makes sense. However, while those are risks, they are indications of fear and catastrophizing and can be better understood by prioritizing facts over fear.

Risk and risk tolerance are felt viscerally and are difficult to define. They possess a "know it when I see it" aspect that is often influenced by irrationality. By objectifying risk it can be appreciated intellectually and managed thoughtfully. Stated differently, a notion of risk that removes emotions and randomness is useful.

Risk in franchising should simply be a measure of certainty, predictability, and consistency of return within a franchise system. In other words, lower variability in expected return correlates with reduced risk and the higher return variability connotes greater risk.

In this context, lower risk does not mean you will earn more money or cannot fail. Instead, it means that you have increased certainty to perform at the levels of other franchisees. And, assuming the average return is sufficient for you that is precisely what you are seeking.

To illustrate this concept, let's look at two franchisors, both of which have 100 franchisees and a mean (average) franchisee net earnings of $250,000.

Franchise "A" has a tight earnings distribution. Eighty percent of the franchisees earn between $200,000 and $300,000. The balance of franchisees earn a little more or less than that range. Franchise "A" has low risk because the expected outcome is highly likely, consistent, and predictable.

Franchise "B", in contrast, has a highly distributed franchisee earnings profile. Twenty percent of its franchisees earn between $200,000-$300,000. Seventy percent earn less than $100,000 and ten percent earn more than $700,000. Franchise "B" has a highly "randomized" earnings distribution and therefore has significantly more risk.

For most people franchise "A" is the right brand choice. For people with a higher acceptance of risk and volatility AND who are exceedingly comfortable with the business model's match to their skills and abilities, franchise "B" may also be a good choice.

This is the foundational concept in understanding franchise risk. Mean, average, or median return are not nearly as relevant as the distribution that leads to those numbers. Franchise financial representations vary greatly and some brands are truly scattershot and randomized.

Again, not all franchisors are created equal. Some have stronger business models, systems, marketing, support, and leadership than others. Some franchisor's success rates significantly outstrip their peers, while others have staggering failure rates.

Overall success rates in franchising mean absolutely nothing to you. What matters is the risk profile of the franchise brand you are considering. Do your research, discern the brand's true risk profile, and match it to yours.

## Franchise Features That Reduce Risk

It is especially important to evaluate franchisor features that increase the predictability of return. Focus on the attributes and features that make performance simpler, more consistent, and allow franchisees to execute on the business plan. It's precisely those business traits that mitigate risk and improve outcomes.

The following franchise business features permit franchisees to focus on execution. Innovative franchisors are constantly iterating their businesses, creating more formulaic models that improve performance and reduce risk.

**Brand lead generation:** Franchisor marketing and lead generation is the most important feature that a franchise can offer to drive performance. Lead generation is multi-faceted. Leads can be generated through social media, google ad words, website spend, or with more traditional marketing methods. The key component of brand lead generation is that the franchisor is using its proven expertise to fill the top of the sales funnel, and provide franchisees with regular insight into marketing performance.

In my experience, filling the top of the sales funnel is the most significant factor in business success or failure and therefore the greatest variable in performance predictability. Unless you have strong sales DNA and/or a remarkably deep network you should seek a brand with strong lead generation.

**Call Centers:** Call centers help franchisees in a number of important ways. First, a call center significantly leverages the franchisee's time by managing calls and administrative tasks. Second, a call center allows the brand to deliver a professional and consistent client experience. Calls are never missed and always handled in a timely professional manner. This is a huge competitive advantage over mom and pop businesses.

Call centers take all different forms with some, in addition to managing incoming client interest, proactively calling potential clients, others scheduling and confirming appointments, while still others will conduct sales on behalf of franchisees. In all incarnations, call centers proffer a huge benefit to a newly-launched franchisee and help to reduce performance variation.

**Hiring/Staffing Support:** Franchisors offer different levels of staffing support. Some identify, screen, and interview candidates for franchisees, while others offer guidance. Hiring support is more indispensable with brands that require specialized employees or in sectors where staffing is particularly tight or nuanced. Because a franchisee is only as good as their team, leveraging the hiring expertise of the franchisor helps to create a more predictable path to success.

**Ongoing coaching, training, and support:** Franchisors proactively provide initial and ongoing training and support. Some franchisors take this to another level by offering personalized one on one coaching. Coaches speak regularly to franchisees, focusing on troubleshooting practices, and ensuring franchisees don't go down unproductive paths. Coaching quickly corrects and normalizes performance.

## Business Model Simplicity

Franchisees benefit from business models that are simple. Avoid joining a Rube Goldberg franchise. Business simplicity takes many different forms such as lower staffing requirements, less process steps, a short sales cycle, or a simple, redundant supply chain. I am always looking for the simplest business model in each sector, because the simpler the business model the more predictable the performance of franchisees.

## The Greatest Risk Is Not Changing

"Mark, I hate my job but I only have 12 more years to go before I can retire."

"My job will likely put me in an early grave but I don't have the courage to make a change."

"I am meant to be miserable professionally."

These are actual statements people made to me when asked, "are you interested in exploring franchise business ownership?"

These responses illustrate the significant role that inertia plays in human life. Many people feel trapped in their careers, either frozen in place or uncertain how to act, yet they would rather accept a bad situation than "risk" finding a better one. It supports the clarity in Thoreau's words that "the mass of men lead lives of quiet desperation." What he failed to add, though, is that they choose those lives out of fear or absurd misapprehensions.

A favorite aphorism that fuels my decision making is that if a person does not make different choices than absolutely, positively nothing will change. Similarly, the definition of insanity is doing the same thing over and over again expecting different results. You must do different things to get different results!

As Eleanor Roosevelt famously said "No one can make you feel bad without your permission". The corollary is that no one is stuck in a bad situation without their permission.

I understand that change is difficult. I was certainly stuck for a time. The magnetism of the present situation and the repelling force of change conspire to keep people stuck in place. Change is scary but . . .

The greatest risk in our lives is being possessed with feelings of utter helplessness and remaining miserable, unfulfilled, and sad. Nothing can be worse than this. There is a higher risk to remain in a bad situation than there is to accept a different risk as you extricate yourself.

It takes courage to become more than you are, as much as you can be. The opposite of courage keeps us stuck. Fear is the greatest warrior against change. But do not confuse a lack of courage with a lack of choices. You always have a choice. You can always choose how you want to live and what to do with your life.

If you're not happy at work, not fulfilled at work, not satisfied at work then you owe it to yourself to explore business ownership. The real risk in life is the difference between what you're capable of and do not achieve because of fear.

When people tell me that they cannot change and choose to remain stuck I am reminded that the difference between a rut and a grave is a matter of inches. Then I ask two questions.

"What happens with your life if you don't change?"

"Are you willing to remain unhappy?"

Again, choosing to remain unhappy is the greatest risk in life.

# 10
## DUE DILIGENCE

*"Diligence is the mother of good fortune."*

—Benjamin Disraeli,

Former British Prime Minister

Until you engage in the due diligence process, it is difficult to truly understand the different and specific aspects
of a franchise brand. It is important to follow the process to
learn everything necessary. At its core, success as a franchisee
is about following the system. The best outcomes are derived
by sticking to the process.

Once you begin, you will be able to go from start to finish
in eight to twelve weeks. During this time, plan on allocating
3-5 hours a week for conversations with the brands and other
aspects of due diligence. Generally, you will have one call
every week with each franchisor. This will keep the process
moving forward at an efficient pace and ensure that another
potential franchisee is not awarded the territory because they
moved faster than you. Unfortunately, this is not an uncom-
mon occurrence for candidates who choose to move slowly.

Each franchise has a clear structure to their due diligence process and every step is designed to lead you through an effective and systematic approach to discovery. The order and cadence of the steps will vary by brand, but here are the areas it will cover:

- Introductory call. This call is an opportunity for you and the franchise developer to build rapport.

- Business basics. Overview of the brand's marketing, sales, operations, real estate (if a retail location is required), products and services, technology, hiring, training and support, financials, and so on.

- Franchise Disclosure Document (FDD) review.

- Territory mapping and discussion. This is when you learn about the geography, demographics and other key facets of a proposed territory.

- Validation. This is when you speak with current franchisees who share their experiences.

- Discovery day. When you meet face to face with the key players at the franchise.

- Contract review. When you review the franchise agreement.

The franchisor shares a ton of information with you because they want you to make an informed decision. Let me suggest a way of managing the information.

**The Perfect Franchise Six-Factor Analysis**

Choosing the perfect franchise is the result of a rigorous, thoughtful, and structured due diligence. My candidates explore individual franchises through adherence to The Perfect Franchise Six-Factor Analysis. These six factors will enable you to gather and track information, recognize areas for additional learning, and allow for final brand analysis and assessment. These are the decision points that will determine if a brand is The Perfect Franchise for you.

**The Six Factors**

*1. How do I get customers?*

A great business model is nothing without customers. This factor addresses the brand's customer acquisition strategy and lead generation. It is important for you to understand the sales and marketing methodology, your role, cost, etc. Questions include:

- What does the lead generation system look like?

- Is there a clear and predictable procedure for lead generation?

- How does the franchisor drive customers?

- What is the franchisee's role in customer acquisition?

- What is the cost of gaining a customer?

- What are the key elements that maximize the sales and marketing process?

- Ultimate question: Am I, as the franchisee, comfortable with the customer acquisition and lead generation process the brand provides?

### 2. How do I serve my customers?

Once customers express an interest, you must deliver your product or service at a high level. This factor focuses on how you can maximize your business' operations. Areas of exploration are hiring, training, supply chain, vendors, etc. Questions include:

- What franchisor support is provided for hiring, training, and managing staff?

- What does the supply chain look like?

- Who are the suppliers?

- What are the factors that can improve a franchisee's operations?

- What are the operational challenges in the system?

- What are the operational areas of strength?

- Ultimate question: Does the franchisor provide a strong enough support ecosystem for me to succeed?

*3. What is expected of me as the franchisee?*

Before joining a franchise, you need to know what will be expected of you and gain role clarity. Ask questions such as:

- What does a day, week, or month in the life of a franchisee look like?

- What is my expected time commitment?

- Is there flexibility in my schedule?

- What are the franchisee's roles and responsibilities?

- How does the franchisee's role evolve over time?

- What positions can franchisees hire for?

- What are the traits of your most successful franchisees?

- What type of franchisee struggles with this brand?

- Ultimate Question: Do I think the role of a franchisee in this brand is a good match for me?

*4. What do the economics look like?*

Freedom, independence, and being your own boss are great, but you need to make money. It is crucial to understand the investment costs, ongoing expenses, and your income potential. Questions include:

- What is the cost of entry for a franchisee?

- What is the income potential?

- What are the ongoing fees? (e.g., royalties, ad funds, etc.)

This factor also provides the opportunity to dive into the drivers and limiters of financial success in a specific brand. Learn about the key performance indicators (KPIs) and how you can turn the dial to improve financial results. Finally, you will want to model the financials to appreciate the brand's potential. The following questions will enable you to uncover the levers to pull or the dials to turn to maximize revenue and profitability once you join a franchise.

- What are the things you do to maximize the impact of your marketing spend?

- What aspects of the sales cycle are the most critical? How do you optimize them?

- How do you manage staffing levels to ensure you are appropriately staffed?

- Do you actively use all the square footage of your location or could you generate as much revenue with a smaller footprint? (minimizing fixed real estate costs is a great way to lower expenses)

- What are the KPIs that drive revenue and what are top performing franchisee's doing to maximize revenue?

- What are the KPIs that drive expenses and what are top performing franchisee's doing to minimize expenses?

- Do you have a pro-forma you can share?

- Ultimate Question: Can this franchise meet my financial expectations?

5. *What is the brand's unique value proposition to a franchisee?*

My clients are sought-after by franchise brands. They are high potentials with the commitment, focus, and skills to succeed in franchising. I share this confidence with my clients, so they approach the due diligence process with a mindset of self-assurance. Yet, there are bumps in the road for all franchisees, and it is important for you to clarify how the franchisor will help you through them. You want to ensure that the franchisor is a true partner. Questions include:

- How will you support me to scale the business?

- How do you help me when challenges arise?

- What are the aspects of the business where new franchisees struggle?

- What can I do proactively to avoid those struggles?

- Ultimate Question: Is the franchisor going to be my partner and support me through thick and thin?

## 6. What is the unique value proposition to customers?

In any business there will be competitors. What is important is joining a business that is differentiated and able to gain market share. Generally, it is not the product or service that is differentiated but how it is delivered. Understand how the value proposition is articulated in marketing, at the point of sale, and how it manifests itself in the customer experience. Questions include:

- Who is the competition?

- How is the brand different from competitors?

- How is that distinction articulated in marketing materials? During the sales process?

- How does the customer experience the difference?

- Ultimate Question: Is the franchisor's value proposition powerful and will it enable me to grow a strong business?

During due diligence, I revisit these six factors often with clients. During those discussions we explore concerns. If there are none, the process continues forward.

## How to Handle Bumps in the Due Diligence Road

It is important to know that the due diligence process always has bumps in it. Let's examine further what to do when an issue arises.

First, pinpoint the issue and define its significance. This simple step often resolves points because they are insignificant.

For substantive items, I advise my clients to speak with the franchisor only after they know precisely how they want it resolved. This is crucial because too often candidates identify areas of concern but don't think about what a resolution looks like. That places an unfair onus on the franchisor to guess what the candidate wants.

Once the issue, its importance, and proposed resolution are defined I discuss with my client the best way of presenting it to the franchisor. This approach provides the franchisor with a clear understanding and roadmap on how to proceed. If the issue is a deal breaker for the candidate then they need to move on and find another franchise brand. If, on the other hand, it is a nice to have but not a need to have, the process moves forward.

The entire purpose of a due diligence process is to gather, analyze, and assess all the information necessary to make an informed decision, and The Perfect Franchise Six-Factor Analysis provides a framework to make that a reality!

**Due Diligence Preparation**

Preparation is very important during due diligence for two reasons. First, it will help you to learn everything you need to know about the franchise. Second, it will position you as a candidate whom brands will covet. Franchise developers can quickly distinguish between top candidates and those who are wasting their time.

Preparation can take many forms and may include franchisor "homework." These assignments are meant to prepare you for the next call and educate you on the brand. They can include documents to review, group calls to attend, videos to watch, or forms to complete. As you are assessing the franchisor, they are doing the same with you, and there is no reason not to put your best foot forward.

Be prepared to have at least two or three calls with each franchisor prior to deciding to end the due diligence with them. The reason for multiple calls is that it is extremely difficult to assess an opportunity quickly. It no longer surprises me when a client who did not want to continue due diligence with a brand eventually joins them!

The franchise developer will be looking for red flags that can disqualify you as a candidate. Some of the big ones are:

- Being late for or missing calls. It is okay to reschedule a call but do it in advance. Be respectful of their time.

- Not asking questions can indicate a lack of interest or engagement. At every step of the process there are myriad opportunities to ask questions and learn more about the brand. Questions come in many forms, including clarification, requests for additional information, or expressions of concern.

- Not viewing videos or reviewing documents shared with you. Again, if you cannot get this done in the allotted timeline, communicate that fact. Communication is simple yet important. Not completing tasks is not an option if you want to join a franchise.

- Failure to complete the franchise application or acknowledge receipt of the FDD. These are non binding but integral steps in your candidacy as a franchisee. Without the application, you will not be awarded a franchise, and without acknowledging the FDD, you cannot accept. These are big red flags for franchisors.

While these concepts appear obvious, people often take things for granted and do not put their best foot forward. Do not put yourself in the position where the franchisor decides you are not right for the brand. Instead, put yourself in the position so that at the end of the process, you are the one with the power to make the decision.

During due diligence, I speak regularly with you and the franchisor to ensure the process is moving smoothly. If there are bumps in the road, I will coach you to stay on track and advise you on how to continue effectively in the process. I speak to you on a weekly basis during due diligence, providing tools and insights to help you maximize each stage of the process. I also perform a lot of tasks behind the scenes to keep the process moving and position you well. But at the end of the day, you are the one responsible for driving the process.

When you enter due diligence, you will be excited and nervous. That is natural. The wonderful thing about franchise exploration is that it is designed to answer all questions and address your concerns systematically so you can make an informed and educated decision.

During the due diligence you will speak to the franchisors, review documents like the FDD, and validate with franchisees. Each of these resources will share information as they see fit. But you want to be the one driving the bus, and the only way you can do that is by asking good questions. What I have provided below is a list of questions to ask franchisors and franchisees.

In addition, though the FDD is a rich document, you need to ask questions to better understand and clarify the information it provides. As you go through the FDD, be sure to write down questions about anything you don't understand, think you understand but are not 100 percent sure of, don't like, or are excited about. With those questions in hand, your FDD review with the franchisor will be productive. Do not make assumptions about meanings. Ask the franchisor to address all your questions.

The franchise due diligence and discovery process starts with an initial call with the franchisor. As I mentioned earlier, beginning at this moment you must put your best foot forward.

The typical first call has a simple and informal cadence and takes between thirty and sixty minutes, although every brand does things a little differently. After you exchange pleasantries, the franchisor will likely ask you about your background, what made you interested in franchising, and why you are interested in that franchise. Then they will either share with you an overview of the brand or ask you if you have any specific questions about the concept. I always encourage you to ask the franchisor to share an overview of the brand because it is important to hear about the business from the franchisor's perspective.

## Questions for Franchisors

- *Can you break down all the costs to purchase the franchise?* This can be found in item 7 of the FDD, but I still encourage you to ask the question. Follow up by asking about the average cost of entry and any cost variables that might exist. For example, there are occasionally geographic variables that need to be accounted for.

- *What are the expectations of a franchisee (roles, responsibilities, skills, and time commitment)?*

- *What are your initial support, training, and grand opening plans?*

- *What type of ongoing support, training, and coaching do you provide?*

- *What are the key traits that lead to franchisee success in your system?*

- *What are the KPIs? How do I turn the dial to increase performance?*

- *What support do you provide to a franchisee who is struggling?*

- *What do you see as the challenges in this market?*

- *What are the opportunities in the market?*

- *What is your unique value proposition?*

## Validation

Validation, speaking to current franchisees, is perhaps the most important aspect of due diligence. You will speak to people who are doing exactly what you are interested in doing.

Franchisees who have already gone through the process will honestly share their experiences, perspectives, and views.

Why are franchisees honest with candidates?

First, brand reputation is very important. Franchisees are very protective of their brands and who joins. They want to tell you the truth so that only strong potential franchisees join. They want the brand to grow with the right people.

Franchisees are not paid or coached on what to say. I once joined an organization (not a franchise) where the interviewers/validators were paid and coached about what to say. When I found out, I was livid and left the organization. Franchising is different. Franchisees spend their time with you because they care. No other reason.

Franchisees are the boots on the ground. They can tell you more about the day-to-day operation of the brand than perhaps anyone else. They run their businesses and know all the challenges and opportunities. They know where you should spend your time and where not to. This is huge!

When you validate, it is important to intentionally choose who you are validating with. I encourage you to speak to top performers, mid-level performers, and laggards. This is critical because you want different perspectives. Also, speak to a new franchisee who can discuss the initial training and support.

## Not All Franchisees Are Created Equal

I want to reinforce this point from earlier because it will arise during validation. It is important to recognize there is a lot of variability in franchisee performance in any franchise system. In any leading franchise there will be some people generating significant incomes while others will be struggling. These are peers who have the same franchise model, training, and support but achieve strangely different results. There are numerous reasons for the disparate results.

First, there is much variability in all aspects of human performance, and franchising is no different. For those of you currently working for others, you see this manifest itself every day. Some employees are strong performers, and others are not. The same stratification exists in franchise systems.

The primary driver of franchisee performance is how well the franchisee fits and executes the system. To better explain the concept, let's break franchisees into three groups using a climbing analogy.

The first group is made up of franchisees who are the wrong fit for the concept. These are people who don't match the expectations, skills, or time commitment of the franchise and, therefore, have a hard time succeeding. For example, if sales, operational, or management skills are required and a franchisee lacks them, they will really struggle. This typically represents about 10 to 15 percent of a franchise system. If you are on the wrong mountain you will never reach the desired summit.

The next group is campers. These are people whose performance is capped by a certain income or effort level where they become comfortable. Once they reach that desired level, they "camp" and stop pushing because they are satisfied. This is most people in any franchise system, or really in life. Campers make up about 60 to 70 percent of franchisees. To be clear, being a camper is not bad and most of them are happy. When hiking, campers reach a nice vista, enjoy the views, and are satisfied, but do not achieve the summit.

I work with one franchise system where, through validation, candidates learn that most performers earn between $50,000 and $75,000. For many of us that is a low number, and we would think there is something wrong with that business model. Yet this franchise validates as well, perhaps better, than most. The franchisees are doing the work they want to do and at the level they want to do it. The franchisor puts no pressure on them to perform at a higher level but provides resources for them to grow if they so choose. In other words, the franchisees are choosing to perform exactly how they want to, and they are a happy and satisfied group!

There are different levels of campers, from the more passive, who camp early, to aggressive ones who push but still stop when satisfied.

Climbers make up the final group. This group is at the top because of the confluence of motivation, skills, and alignment with the franchise. They don't stop until they are the top performers in any franchise system. They are motivated by achievement. They make up between 20 and 25 percent of any franchise system. In climbing, these are the folks who fight to reach the summit.

Here are a few ways to use this construct.

First, let's revisit knowing yourself. Introspection is important to figuring out whether franchising is right for you, and if it is, what the best franchise will be. Once again, this is based on fit.

Second, when you go through validation and speak to current franchisees, use this idea to validate the quality of the system, not the franchisee you are speaking with. Stay focused on the franchise system's training, support, product, and service and not the franchisee's performance. To be clear, validation is learning about the franchise system and not the performance of the franchisee.

I smile when I get calls from clients during validation saying they want to move ahead after speaking to a franchisee who is doing well. I always ask, "What does their performance have to do with yours? If you spoke to a poor performer, would you jettison the brand? Focus on the system!"

Look for patterns. Learn how most franchisees feel about the support the franchisor provides. Remember that franchisees are business owners and are taking time out of their day to speak with you. Be respectful of their time and appreciate that not all will be in talkative moods. There are sample questions below to assist you in preparation for these calls.

Once again, anything you learn through franchisee conversations, the internet, and so on that creates unease or uncertainty should be addressed with the franchisor. They can often confirm or allay concerns easily.

The best way to start these calls is by thanking the franchisees for their time. Let franchisees know you appreciate them, their time, and candor. This approach is not only appropriate but will start the call on the right track.

Your goal is to figure out where your performance will be in a franchise based on the support and systems they provide. That is the important piece of information. People gravitate to the performance levels they want or are capable of achieving. In any leading franchise system performance comes down to the franchisee, and a person's results are based on their skills, strengths, and motivation.

### Sample Questions for Franchisees

These questions should serve as a general guide as you validate with franchisees. I encourage you to create a list of questions that address all the areas you want to learn about.

Validation Questions

- What did you do prior to franchising? The purpose of this question is to see if there are similarities between your respective backgrounds.

- Why did you choose to join this franchise?

- What skills do you think are important for franchisees to have?

- What was the real estate support like (for brick and mortar only)?

- What are the biggest challenges in the business?

- How do you hire employees/contractors?

- When you started, were there any unforeseen expenses?

- Did the initial training prepare you for opening?

- What is the biggest mistake that a new franchisee can make?


Support

- How was the initial training? Did it prepare you for opening?

- What does ongoing support and training look like?

- Are there advanced training programs, webinars, and conferences?

- Who do you call for questions and advice? Are they helpful?

### Marketing Programs

- How does the franchisor support your marketing?

- What lead-generation programs does the franchisor have? What is the return on investment (ROI)?

- Who are your competitors? How do you articulate your competitive advantage?

### Technology

- Does the technology platform allow you to run your business effectively?

- What types of technology systems are provided?

### Franchisor-Franchisee Relations

- Is the franchisor easy to work with?

- How are disagreements resolved?

Owner's Role

- What does a day in the life of a franchisee look like?

- What separates the top performers from others?

Earnings

- What are your annual earnings?

- What is your net?

KPIs

This should be focused on what you are measuring and how to improve performance.

- What are the KPIs?

- What are the key factors that impact both gross and net?

- How do you track metrics (system, frequency, and so on)?

- How do you turn the dial to improve performance?

## Discovery Day

Discovery day is essentially the final interview. The entire franchise discovery process from the first communication with the franchisor is basically a long interview process. They are deciding whether you can succeed in their franchise, and you are deciding if it is the right fit.

Discovery day historically has been an in-person event, but some brands have transitioned to conducting virtual discovery days. Either way, the franchisor invites serious candidates they believe are good matches for their brand to learn more about the franchise system.

While not all franchises have discovery days, this is typically the last phase prior to being awarded a franchise.

Discovery day allows you to fine-tune your understanding of the franchise, learn about its values and beliefs, and see firsthand what makes them successful. Most importantly, it lets you meet your potential franchise partners, allowing for the creation of deeper, more personal relationships. Finally, both parties can gauge levels of interest and address concerns.

If you land a discovery day invite, the franchisor will expect that you:

- Understand the franchisor business model

- Know the responsibilities of a franchisee

- Have reviewed the FDD

- Have validated with several existing franchisees

- Are seriously considering joining the franchise

Mutual interest and your knowledge of the brand sets up

the discovery day as one of the final steps in your decision-making process.

Franchisors award franchises to candidates who are passionate, committed to following the brand's systems and processes, have the skills and commitment necessary to succeed, and have the values to embrace the culture.

When you reach discovery day, both you and the brand already like each other. D-day is more about cultural fit and how you and the team click. Here are some tips to leave discovery day with an offer to join:

- Show up on time, and that means five or ten minutes early. Stay during all the presentations and chat with the franchisor's staff during breaks. Show genuine interest!

- Attend with your business partner or spouse if they will be involved in the business.

- Ask questions. Nothing shows interest more than a few good questions.

- Find out everything you need and whether you connect with the leadership team and staff. Be prepared to decide whether or not you want to move forward with the franchise.

- Stay engaged. Listen actively. Follow along in your book during presentations and take notes. Turn your phone off and avoid distractions.

- During all meals and events, it is important to be personable, interested, and engaged. Don't have more than one drink, eat politely, and be kind to the staff. Everything matters when you are trying to make a strong impression.

Franchisors typically want you to digest the information and allow time for you to decide. That said, you will be expected to decide shortly after attending discovery days. If you are awarded a franchise at discovery day, thank them, and let them know that you want to review the opportunity with your family.

# 11

# THE FRANCHISE DISCLOSURE DOCUMENT (FDD)

*"The length of this document defends it well against the risk of being read."*

—Winston Churchill

The Federal Trade Commission (FTC) requires that franchise candidates receive information to make educated decisions in the purchase of a franchise. A key regulatory component is the FDD. The FDD is fundamentally a franchise offering memorandum that contains twenty-three items or sections. Each item is essentially an informational area that a candidate would want to learn about. The FDD is long—often a few hundred pages—but it is written in plain English. It is a crucial step in the due diligence process.

Candidates must receive the FDD, and acknowledge receipt of it, at least fourteen days prior to signing a franchise agreement. The FTC does this to ensure that candidates, once they receive FDDs, have an appropriate amount of time to digest and understand the information. The fourteen-day clock begins ticking when item 23 of the FDD is signed. It is important to note that signing this FDD receipt does not create any commitment or obligation.

The FDD is written by the franchisor's attorneys and, therefore, is skewed toward the franchisor. For example, you may find ten pages on how a franchisor can terminate a franchise agreement but only a paragraph on how you can. The purpose of the FDD, in addition to educating candidates, is to protect the franchisors and existing franchisees. The FDD is written to safeguard the brand and the best interests of successful owners. When read from this perspective, it appears much more palatable.

It is akin to having a homeowner's association. When you buy a house with an association and read the document, you learn about all the things you cannot do, such as the colors you cannot paint your house or the vehicles you cannot park in your driveway. However, when you drive through a community with a homeowner's association and then one without the association, you see the difference. No trailers in the driveways, no peeling paint, and no overgrown grass. That is why the franchisors write FDDs to protect the brand and ultimately, if you join, your interests.

**A Few Tips on Reading an FDD**

First, understand that the FDD will not tell you how to be successful. I recommend reading it only after you understand all aspects of the business model, including marketing, product/service, support, and technology. Get comfortable with the franchisor. Too often candidates read the FDD early in the process, and if not ready, it is a mistake. Franchisors can get excited when they find strong candidates and send the FDD out too soon. If you are not ready for it, don't review it. Simply tell the franchisor that you are interested in learning a bit more before focusing on the FDD.

Second, when you read the FDD, be sure to note anything you would like to discuss with the franchisor. Liberally ask questions, for clarification and more information. Asking questions, and not making assumptions, is extremely important in the due diligence process.

Third, take the perspective of a successful owner, not a candidate. This helps to reframe the FDD into a document that will protect your investment!

Fourth, I recommend you engage a franchise attorney, and I will introduce you to some of the best. Attorney review provides additional understanding of the agreement and puts you at ease. The reality is that the franchisor rarely changes the agreement, but the attorney review will deliver clarity and peace of mind.

Finally, as you begin reviewing the FDD, pay particular attention to the following key sections. These will provide an overview into the financial side and the culture of the brand.

- Item 4: Litigation for the previous 10 years.

- Items 5, 6, and 7: Breakdown of the costs along with a total estimate of expenses.

- Item 19: Earnings claim.

- Item 20: Information on franchise owners, past and present.

**Overview of FDD Items**

*Cover Page*

States that the FTC has not reviewed the document and did not pass on its veracity. It suggests you read the entire document and do your research. It also suggests the FDD and the franchise agreement should be reviewed by an adviser, such as a lawyer or accountant. All of this is good advice.

*Second Page*

Contains a summary of the franchise offering and the investment the franchisee is required to make. It also contains information about risk factors that a franchisee should know before signing a franchise agreement.

*Item 1: Franchisor Information*

Provides an overview of the company and franchise.

*Item 2: Business Experience*

Presents professional information about the franchise and its officers, directors, and executives.

*Item 3: Litigation*

Provides relevant current and past criminal and civil litigation for the franchise and its management. This section must report ten years of litigation.

*Item 4: Bankruptcy*

Discloses information about whether the franchisor or members of its management team have gone through a bankruptcy.

*Item 5: Initial Franchise Fee*

Elucidates the initial fees paid to the franchisor. It identifies what payments the franchisee makes to the franchisor prior to opening the business, and if the fees are not uniform, it provides the factors that determine the variable amount of the fee.

*Item 6: Other Fees*

Details the recurring fees or payments that the franchisee must make to the franchisor, including franchise fee, royalties, advertising, training fees, transfer fees, audit costs, renewal fees, and other miscellaneous fees. This is an important section!

*Item 7: Initial Investment*

A table that includes all the expenditures a franchisee is required to make to establish the franchise. Essentially, this combines item

5 fees with all other fees required for opening a location, such as lease improvements, equipment, grand opening marketing expenses, and so on. The information in this section will help you make an accurate investment estimate.

*Item 8: Restriction on Sources of Products and Services*

Discusses any franchisor restrictions on the suppliers and specification of the products used by the franchisee. Most restrictions that franchisors place on sources and products are to ensure brand consistency and quality. This is particularly important for food franchises.

*Item 9: Franchisee's Obligations*

Identifies the obligations of franchisees. The list informs the franchisee of the obligations, where they can be found elsewhere in the FDD, and where they can be found in the franchise agreement. The details of the obligations are not discussed in item 9. Not all systems have uniform obligations, but it is important to understand what is expected of you.

*Item 10: Financing Available*

Describes the terms and conditions of any financing arrangements offered directly or indirectly by the franchisor.

*Item 11: Franchisor's Obligations*

Lays out the obligations of the franchisor and the ways they are required to support you. It shares pre- and post-opening support and clarifies what you receive for your fees.

*Item 12: Territory*

Defines how territories work within a franchise system, whether they are exclusive, their size, etc.

*Item 13: Trademarks*

Provides the franchisee with information about the franchisor's trademarks, service marks, and trade names.

*Item 14: Patents, Copyrights, and Proprietary Information*

Gives franchisees information about patents or copyrights of the franchisor.

*Item 15: Obligations to Participate in the Actual Operation of the Franchise Business*

Lays out the franchisee's requirements for involvement in operating the franchise. Some franchise systems require franchisees to devote their full time to the operation of the business, while others may allow for semi-absentee ownership or a management structure.

*Item 16: Restrictions on What the Franchise May Sell*

Details any restrictions on the goods and services the franchisee may offer.

*Item 17: Renewal, Termination, Transfers, and Dispute Resolution*

Provides a table about the terms of the agreement. Included in this section is information on things such as:

- The length of the initial term of the agreement and information on renewal periods

- Potential reasons for termination and the termination process

- The franchisor's and the franchisee's rights to transfer or assign the agreement

- Restrictive covenants

- Franchise agreement modification

- Dispute resolution procedures and governing law

*Item 18: Public Figures*

The franchisor discloses the use of any public figure in the franchise system, how much the person is paid, the extent the public figure is involved in the actual management, and the public figure's total investment.

*Item 19: Earnings Claim*

This is the first item that many candidates view because it details the financial performance of their system and provides information that a franchisee can use to estimate earnings. While not required, the item 19 disclosure may include levels or ranges of actual or potential sales, costs, income, or profits for franchised or non franchised locations. There is a lot of variability in franchisee performance, so no one can tell you how much money you will make. But item 19 provides information to help you build a pro forma balance sheet.

*Item 20: List of Franchise Outlets*

Offers information about the locations operated in the system. It includes information such as:

- The number of franchises and company-owned locations by state.

- The names, addresses, and telephone numbers of franchisees.

- The estimated number of franchises to be sold in the next year.

- The number of franchises transferred, canceled, or terminated.

- The number of franchises that have not been renewed or have been reacquired by the franchisor.

The franchisor is required to provide contact information for every franchisee who has been terminated, canceled, not renewed, or who otherwise ceased doing business under the franchise agreement during the past year. This provides the necessary information to estimate the success rate for franchisees.

*Item 21: Financial Statements*

Includes audited financial statements for the past three years or for a shorter period if the franchisor has not been in business for three years.

*Item 22: Contracts*

A list of the franchise agreement or license agreement and all other related agreements that the franchisee will be required to sign. These agreements must be attached as exhibits to the FDD.

*Item 23: Receipt*

Candidates are required to sign a receipt that they received the FDD if they want to eventually purchase a franchise. The signature does not commit the signatory and is a simple acknowledgement that it was received. Two copies of the receipt form are provided in item 23.

# 12

# FINANCIALS: HOW TO AFFORD A FRANCHISE

*"Never say you cannot afford something. That is a poor man's attitude. Ask HOW to afford it."*

—Robert Kiyosaki, Author of *Rich Dad Poor Dad*

I always loved the Kiyosaki quote because it is a seminal truth. You can make anything that you want enough a reality; it is just a matter of how. Franchises are not free and as you learn about franchising, it is important to simultaneously consider the financial side of the equation. You may learn that you need to be in a better financial position to join a franchise. If that is the case do not fret it. Just start saving for the future!

A simple framework to understand the financial aspects of franchising is to focus on three variables:

- Franchise investment range and living expenses

- Income potential and cash flow timeline of the franchise

- Funding options

## Franchise Investment and Living Expenses

Assess your ability to fund and finance a franchise early in the process because it impacts the franchise brands that could be the right fit and how you can scale. I refer you to one of my franchise funding partners, who are able to provide an understanding of potential options and cost of capital, and then lay out the steps in the franchise funding process. Most importantly, the finance experts make it easy to navigate the funding process and guide you to the best options.

There are multiple variables in the funding process such as liquidity, net worth, and credit score. Therefore, it is important that you understand the different choices available so you can make an informed decision.

The number one reason businesses fail is because they are undercapitalized. In other words, they run out of money before they make enough to pay their bills from business earnings. Franchises help to ameliorate that issue by clearly defining the amount of capital it takes to launch the business.

With the financial visibility provided by the brands, I recommend mapping out a clear plan on how you are going to pay all business expenses during the ramp-up stage. In addition, create a plan for paying your personal living expenses for the first year. Regardless of the quality of a franchise or your ability to operate it at a high level, I implore you to be conservative, so you have ample capital for your professional and personal needs.

Franchisors do a solid job of putting minimum financial requirements, such as net worth and liquidity, in place for candidates. While these are helpful guideposts for you, they are not exact. Every person and family has unique financial situations, and only you truly know yours.

As you begin exploring franchising, take a financial inventory. Estimate your net worth by assessing your assets and deducting liabilities. Assets include:

- Cash

- Stocks, bonds, mutual funds, and other non-real estate investments

- Home/real estate value

- Retirement accounts (for example, 401k, 403b, IR A)

- Cars, motorcycles, mobile homes, and boats

- Miscellaneous personal property

Next, list and subtract your liabilities. These include:

- Mortgages

- Credit card debt

- Lines of credit/auto debt

- Accounts payable

It is also important to understand your personal cash

flow—essentially a cash in, cash out analysis. This is especially important if you plan on leaving your job and will no longer have that income stream to pay your living expenses. Franchisees need to be able to simultaneously fund the franchise and their lives. Inability to do both will lead to difficulties up to and including failure.

Possessing a strong understanding of your financial situation will help you plan appropriately for weathering any challenges.

**How Much Money Can I Make?**

While the desire for happiness, freedom, independence, and control are important reasons people join franchises, income potential is perhaps of supreme importance. No one would ever join a business or take a job if they could not earn a good living. However, franchisors are restricted by the FTC on making any earnings statements outside of item 19. In practice, that means you need to explore item 19s, validate with franchisees, and create financial models to gain clarity about income potential and cash flow.

In general, the best way to do this is by using the item 19 and validation calls to understand gross revenue ranges, expenses (for example, salaries and marketing), and margins. With this information you can create an Excel spreadsheet that lays out all the variables and options. While this may sound complicated, it is pretty simple. A tip is to ask newer franchisees if they created a pro forma that they are willing to share. This can be a good head start. Be sure to ask about the accuracy and what changes, based on their experience, they would suggest.

Create a range of financial outcomes. Begin by modeling what you project, from research, to be the "average" level of revenue and income you anticipate earning. Average does not mean brand average, rather it is the earnings (gross and net) you expect to generate from your research. Remember, your performance is based on you and not that of other franchisees.

Next, create an upper and lower range by using a percentage variable. In other words, take the original "average" and factor it lower AND higher by 10, 15, or even 25 percent. Now you have an upper and lower limit range of reasonably expected performance.

An important consideration when you are assessing income is that business owners are afforded opportunities to reduce their tax burden in ways that employees are not. When validating, ask about "owner benefit" and not salary. Business expenses like a home office, equipment (computers, furniture, cell phones), utilities, internet, automobiles, etc. may be deductible business expenses offsetting personal ones and creating owner benefits. Of course, you will need to consult your tax adviser about your specific situation.

## Funding Options

Now let's turn our attention to the numerous funding options available for franchises. Rates, ratios, and program terms change frequency, so it is important to use this for general purposes, as it is not necessarily dispositive of all the programs available.

*Self-Funding*

Depending on your financial means and the initial investment, you may very well have the capital to pay for the total investment and can consider self-funding. This is a great option if you have the financial ability to fully fund and you do not like debt. If you are someone who paid off your mortgage as quickly as possible for peace of mind, I am talking to you!

Simply having the ability to fully fund does not mean it is the right decision. Conduct a simple cost-benefit analysis and take stock of what you could do with the money if you chose to borrow instead of self-fund. For example, you could buy stocks, bonds, real estate, or even another franchise.

If you don't have the capital to fully fund or want to use other people's money, read on! The following are the possible lending options available.

*Retirement Accounts (ROBS)*

Rollover for Business Startup Loans (ROBS) allow you to

use your retirement funds on a tax free and penalty free basis to finance your franchise. Basically, you engage a qualified intermediary to use your retirement accounts to fund your franchise. The mechanics are that you create a C Corp, place it in the retirement account, and buy the shares with your corporation. This is a popular option but can only be done with funds that are not in your current employer's retirement plan.

### Small Business Administration (SBA) Loans

The SBA is a government agency dedicated to funding small businesses, recognizing they are the lifeblood of the economy. Lenders provide these loans, and a portion of each loan is guaranteed by the government, thus reducing the risk to the lender. Because the risk is reduced by the government guarantee, lenders can provide lower interest rates and better terms.

The SBA is the go-to resource for potential franchisees. Typically, the SBA provides competitive rates and ratios. While not a steadfast rule, good credit is typically required to qualify. SBA loans generally have ten-year terms and amortization periods.

### Banks

Banks provide term loans and lines of credit. When you receive a term loan, you get a lump sum of capital and need to pay it back, with interest, over the term of the loan. By way of reference, a home mortgage is a term loan. A line of credit is a fund that you can tap into on an as-needed basis. You only pay interest on a line of credit when you use it.

Banks will assess your creditworthiness and decide if you are a good risk. The stronger your credit and higher your net worth, the better rates and terms you will receive. It is also important to note that banks provide the best lending terms to their existing customers. If you have a strong relationship with a bank, you may have access to more competitive rates than if you randomly shop banks. So, start with your current bank.

*Friends and Family Financing*

Friends and family financing is when people you know invest in your company. It is a common way of launching a business. While iterations include taking a loan, receiving a gift, or bringing in a friend or family member as a partner, the common thread is that the terms are generally favorable for the franchisee.

A potential drawback is that if there are any issues, they can become personal and impact friendships or family relationships. To ensure no issues arise, discuss the risks of any new business with them, and draft an agreement that defines the terms—just like you would for any other lending source. A positive benefit of this is that you have other people vested in the success of your franchise.

*Franchisor Financing*

Some franchise brands provide in-house financing. These are typically highly customized programs designed for their franchise. Some of these programs use the franchisors' capital to finance, while others leverage relationships with third-party funders. These programs rely on the success of their brand to create a financing option for new franchisees and are based more on the franchise's creditworthiness than that of the franchisees. Terms of in-house financing programs differ greatly. These programs make financing easy with their one-shop approach.

# 13

# FREQUENTLY ASKED QUESTIONS— AND THE ANSWERS!

*"He who is not everyday conquering some fear has not learned the secret of life."*

—Ralph Waldo Emerson

### Are All Franchises Created Equal?

No! Some brands are fabulous and others are not. When comparing brands, there are often crucial differentiators in the business model, product/service, and support that impact the ability of the franchisees to succeed and scale.

Franchises succeed or fail because of the quality of their systems. That is the area you want to kick the tires on. Use The Perfect Franchise Six-Factor Analysis (Chapter 10) and validate to understand the processes and their quality.

It is difficult for candidates to identify the best brands in every franchise sector. I cannot stress the importance of speaking to a franchise consultant who will identify the finest franchisors in each sector.

**Do Franchisees Always Succeed?**

There are significant performance differences between franchisees. So no, not all franchisees succeed.

Think of franchisee performance like a bell curve. Most franchisees are doing fine, the top franchisees are crushing it, and the bottom are struggling. Your objective during due diligence and validation is to thoroughly understand the business model, its drives, who succeeds, and who struggles. If you don't think you will be in the top 50% of franchisees, then that concept is not for you.

**Will I Lose My Individuality in a Franchise?**

While you will follow the franchisor's business model, you will be able to create the culture and customize your business through the products or services offered, marketing strategies, hiring, and management. Some brands allow more customization than others. For example, McDonalds or Dunkin are going to be turnkey systems with little variability. That is what customers have come to expect from them. In contrast, home service brands will have more flexibility.

Make no mistake about it: Franchisees run their own businesses and put their signatures on them.

## Do Franchises Provide Everything Needed?

From a business model and support standpoint, they do. Franchises offer systems, processes, support, training, coaching, real estate services, and marketing.

Franchisees must bring work ethic, drive, motivation, and people skills.

## Are Franchises More Expensive than Starting Your Own Business?

There are fees associated with franchise ownership. Many of those fees are for items that you will need in any business. The financial benefit of franchising is that it reduces expenses by superior processes, improved purchasing power, and centralized support. The efficient nature of the franchise model, higher success rates, and scalability ensure that the better franchises are not more expensive than starting your own business.

## Can't I Just Find a Franchise on My Own?

Yes, you can. You can do a google search or go to a franchise portal and find brands. However, if you want to optimize your decision, this is not the best approach.

There are thousands of franchises available in the United

States. But not all of them provide strong business models and support. In addition, it is easy to get excited about a concept that is not right for you. An interesting fact is that over 75 percent of people who invest in a franchise choose one not originally considered. Using an experienced franchise consultant increases your chances of finding the right franchise, and our services are provided at no cost to you.

This is a big decision in your life. Maximize your chances of success.

## Does Franchising Take the Fear Out of Business Ownership?

Noooooooo! There is always fear when you change directions, start a new endeavor, and leave your comfort zone. However, franchising provides the comfort of knowing you are supported by a team vested in your success, and you are part of a proven system. Manage your fear with the tips discussed in Chapter 2.

## What Support Will the Franchisor Provide?

Franchisors provide significant levels of initial and ongoing support. Perhaps the most important support they provide is psychological. Knowing that you have a proven model, strong marketing, operations, and training provides a needed confidence boost because executing a system is easier than creating one.

Some of the key components of the franchise support model include:

Prelaunch:

- Proven business model and operation playbook

- In-house or preferred financing partners

- Pre Opening support

- Site selection and negotiation support (if brick and mortar is required)

- Design and construction guidance (if brick and mortar is required)

- Training and coaching online, in the classroom, and/or in the field

- Grand opening or launch programs centered on marketing and preparedness

Ongoing support:

- Training, coaching, and conferences

- Support and sharing of best practices with franchisees

- Turnkey marketing system and execution

- Interaction and improvements from other franchisees

- Constantly improving model

- Proven operating system and manual

- Proactive and reactive coaching and support

- Lower costs of products and services based on large purchasing power

Franchisors will support franchisees in all ways necessary and appropriate. They are committed to their franchisees because that is how they succeed. Franchisees buy into a franchise for the systems and processes, and by executing them in the manner laid out, maximize their chances of achievement.

A franchisor does not know when franchisees need help. As a franchisee, you need to proactively avail yourself of the franchisor's support. The best franchisees ask the most questions and seek the most support. Ask and you will receive!

## Why Do Franchisees Fail?

An extremely high percentage of franchisees are happy and achieve their personal and professional goals. But not all franchisees succeed. Indeed, part of my role as a franchise consultant is to help you understand if you are a good fit for franchising or a particular franchise.

From my experience, here are the top reasons franchisees fail:

1.  They do not want to own a business. To succeed in anything, you need to have a deep desire, and sometimes

franchisees are not fully committed to being their own bosses and running a business. The decision to launch a business can have a profound impact on your personal, professional, and financial life, and as such, should not be taken lightly. Franchising is not a way to alleviate or escape a bad career or a nasty boss.

2. Low commitment or effort. Whether you are going into franchising full-time or keeping your day job, you must prepare to commit the hours necessary to the endeavor or hire a strong manager early in the process. There is a negative correlation in any business between time and money. The more time you spend, the less money it costs to run the business because you are doing the work instead of hiring someone. But if you do not have the time, spend the money so that someone does. It is important during due diligence to understand completely what is expected of you and the effort needed to achieve your goals.

3. Skill deficits. While the requisite skills vary by brand, communications, management, operations, sales, and time management are important for many brands. The areas in which I witness the greatest skills deficits are in management and sales. For example, a franchisee lacking sales skills may not be able to attract customers, and one devoid of management skills cannot properly hire employees and service customers. During discovery, find out what the necessary key skills are, and be

honest with yourself about whether you possess them.

4. Undercapitalization. Running a business requires more financial wherewithal than the initial capital investment. Working capital is crucial until the franchise turns cash flow positive. Lack of working capital can be caused by starting on a shoestring, not understanding the cash requirements, a slow launch, or the franchise not suggesting enough money in the Franchise Disclosure Document (FDD). During validation, ask franchisees how much money is needed and if there were any unforeseen expenses or cash flow issues.

5. Failure to follow the model. Franchisees invest in a proven business model, systems, and processes. Funny thing is that not all franchisees follow the plan. Poor execution dooms many businesses. Some franchisees think they can do it better and eschew the tried-and-true methods. Because they are not executing the plan, their odds of success drop precipitously. The solution is simple: Follow the plan!

6. Choosing the wrong franchise. Clients often want a particular concept because they personally love a brand or think it is a cool business. However, there is a profound difference between having a strong affinity for a brand and operating that business. You can avoid this pitfall by matching your personal and professional interests and skills to the franchise. During

due diligence learn what a "day in the life" looks like. If you are not comfortable and excited to do the necessary tasks, it is probably not the right fit.

7. Bad franchise model. All franchisee failures are not their own fault. Franchisees expect a strong business model, training, support, and so on, but if you choose a weak brand, you will not get that. All franchisors are not created equal. You can protect yourself in a couple of ways. First, review the FDD to see how many franchisees failed. A high percentage of failures is a red flag, but give the franchisor the opportunity to explain it. Also, drill down into the training and support while conducting due diligence and validation.

## Should I Buy a Franchise or a Non-Franchise Business?

A major benefit and differentiator of franchising versus non-franchised business opportunities is that the Federal Trade Commission (FTC) regulates franchising, and the regulations are in place to protect the franchisee. The government requires numerous disclosures and regulates how, when, and by whom information can be communicated. Franchising is a much more predictable model and much easier to perform due diligence on than business opportunities.

In contrast "business opportunities" often masquerade as franchises, but they are unregulated and can make any claim they want because it does not need to be verified or regulated. The franchise world, with its FDD, is much easier to validate than business opportunities.

## Should I Buy a New or Existing Franchise Unit?

A new franchise unit lets you put your stamp on it immediately. You can build it with your employees, your culture, and your style. New franchise units have better territory availability and allow you a much broader choice of brand options than resales, which have limited availability.

Launching a new unit is much easier than one might think because the franchise has a well-defined business model. Essentially, franchisees need to execute the business plan. New franchise locations can scale quickly and do not come with any built-in headaches from the previous owner.

If you want to grow a business from scratch and follow the model, new units are for you!

When you buy an existing franchise, a lot of the heavy lifting has been done. The business is up and running and there is a customer base to tap into. The initial marketing push is already complete, and there is some brand recognition in the community.

A challenge is that existing franchise locations that are performing strongly are often purchased by other franchisees in that system. This is called "internal franchising." This limits the number and quality of resale franchises.

Depending on the situation, the resale may have problems or reputational issues. While it is not always easy to identify the reasons for the sale of the franchise units you are exploring, it is important to do so. Don't be afraid to ask the franchisee uncomfortable questions, and if the answers are not satisfactory, move on. In addition, an existing franchise business will have more expenses than a new one. That means you need to learn the business quickly.

Costs will vary. Successful resale units will cost more than a new territory, so investment amount is an important consideration. If the resale cost is similar or less than that of a new unit, there is likely a reason you need to understand. While it is always critical to conduct thorough due diligence, there is an additional level required in resales. Not only do you need to learn about the franchise, you also must learn about the existing unit you are buying.

Resales may provide extensive clarity into the financials because you will be able to review the franchisee's existing and historical financials. Depending on how well the franchisor keeps her books, you will gain great insight. Using the financials as guideposts, I suggest comparing the business to others in the franchisor's system. Are they underperforming or outperforming? It is important to know if you are buying a business that you can grow significantly or one that is maxed out. Both have their value depending on business goals.

## How Do I Handle Advice from Friends and Family?

One thing that often arises when you investigate buying a business is that you will receive solicited or unsolicited feedback from others. When you begin talking to your friends and family, they will have opinions.

Clients tell me they had a great call with a friend who knows someone who did well in franchising. Alternatively, they will tell me a family member knows someone who struggled in franchising.

While well meaning, neither comment is helpful in your decision-making process. It does not matter if someone else succeeded or failed in a franchise. What is important is whether *you* can succeed in one of the specific franchises you are exploring. Period.

You are conducting the due diligence and have the facts. If you are going to have someone help you make the decision, it is essential for that person to be part of the process and learn alongside you. Otherwise, that advice is likely not going to be on point.

## Should I Leave My Current Career Path?

This is an incredibly personal decision. Each person I speak with has a different decision tree. And it typically comes down to pain.

Pain points, in this context, are the problems with your current career that you are seeking to solve. Pain creates motivation. Pain varies in terms of degree. With pain points, only you can decide how important they are to solve. For example, for some people, being underappreciated at work is no big deal. For others it is huge. You need to assess how much pain you will put up with.

## What if I Validate With an Unhappy Franchisee?

You may speak to an unhappy franchisee. When you speak with franchisees you are not confirming their performance; you are validating the brand and seeking patterns. Is the unhappy franchisee following the franchise model? Probably not. But if the franchisee says they are following the model, ask why others are succeeding and this franchisee is struggling. Speak to several franchisees and look for a trend of good experiences or bad experiences. You may speak to a bad franchisee; it can happen with any franchise. Look for commonalities.

## What if I Find Something Negative Online?

The internet is not known for its positive posts! You want—need—facts. If something negative arises, make a note of it, and ask the franchisor. If you see something positive online, you should bring it up to the franchisor as well. You want to be open with franchisors about potential negatives and positives.

Do not consider the internet the paragon of accurate information.

## How Do I Handle My Spouse Not Supporting Franchising?

First, you want to stay married. If your spouse says they are not excited about franchising, you must understand why. It may be because of fear, lack of knowledge about the concepts, or another reason. Hopefully you have been engaging your spouse the entire time, and if not, have your spouse speak with your consultant and the brand. Your spouse probably knows less than you about the concept, and therefore has less information and facts to overcome their fears. It is important to ensure that your spouse has the facts!

## What if I Want to See Additional Brands?

You may want to see more brands to ensure you are making the best decision, and believe comparison will help accomplish that. Have two or three calls with each brand before considering additional brands. After that, as you learn more about franchising, your criteria could change. If that happens, you can recalibrate and find additional brands.

## I Think the Royalties Are Too High

Royalty fees do not occur in a vacuum. It is a question of whether the franchisor earns their fees. Part of the due diligence process is to gain an understanding of what the brand provides for its royalties. The easiest way to do that is to understand the business model and speak with their franchisees. Ask several franchisees if they feel the franchisor earns the royalty fees or not. Understand what you get in return.

Sometimes a royalty of 15 percent is a bargain because of an amazing level of franchisor support (call center, billing center, etc.). Other times 3 percent is too much because you receive nothing in return. If franchisees obtain value for their royalties, that's a good thing. If they don't, we'll find other concepts!

## I Can Do This Business Myself

Some clients believe that they can execute a concept as well as the franchisor. That is almost never the case. There are several reasons why the franchise model has greater success and risk is relatively simple to assess.

- Franchises need their franchisees to succeed.

- Franchises have proven business models that are consistent and repeatable. Having a system to launch, grow, and scale a business lowers risk.

- Franchises have FDDs, which provides a ton of information about the franchise.

- You can speak confidentially with other franchise business owners so you can validate what you learned.

- You will receive an operations playbook, training, and support.

Importantly, if you think you can perform better than the franchisor, you should address that with them. Ask them what they do for you and understand the value they can add. If you still cannot find it, then the business is not for you!

# CONCLUSION

*"No man ever steps in the same river twice, for it's not the same river and he's not the same man."*

—Heraclitus, Greek Stoic Philosopher

Writing a book was always on my bucket list. I wrote this book to help you explore franchising. Life is a funny thing though. The book writing process provided me with tremendous personal growth and clarity.

I now view myself as a writer (I hope you do too!). I am already thinking about my next book. The change in self-definition was hugely helpful.

I am on the edge of my river as I write this. It is too cold to step in it, but Heraclitus' lesson remains the same. We are different, forever changing. Curious, restless, excited, enthusiastic, and searching for answers. Hungry to be the best version of ourselves. The realization that we are all on a distinctive journey grows every day.

Every reader will take away different things from this book. What I hope you leave with, more than anything else, is that you are on a unique path. No one can or should tell you what to do.

I am grateful to be able to share meaningful insights with you. Every day, I experience people challenging themselves and striving to improve. I am honored that you are one of them.

Whatever direction you choose, I wish you nothing but the best!

# ABOUT THE AUTHOR

**M**ARK SCHNURMAN is a highly accomplished professional with more than 30 years of corporate and entrepreneurial experience in real estate, financial services, human resources, education, and sales training and consulting. An enthusiastic proponent of entrepreneurship and franchising, he has spent his career developing people and growing organizations. His personal, tailored, passionate approach with clients has enabled his success as one of **America's leading franchise consultants** and founder of **The Perfect Franchise**. Notably, Mark accepted an invitation into the prestigious **Forbes Council** as a contributing expert.

As a franchise consultant, Mark is sought out by professionals, families, and investment groups interested in exploring alternative career opportunities or seeking to build income and wealth through full-time, semi-absentee, and passive concepts.

Mark curates a personalized process to isolate high-potential franchises that match the skills, lifestyle, and financial goals of each client. He then coaches his clients through all aspects of identifying, investigating, and owning a franchise, especially, how to methodically assess and compare opportunities.

Prior to founding The Perfect Franchise, Mark held senior positions at several real estate and financial institutions, and owned various businesses. A noted speaker and author, Mark holds a JD from The Ohio State University and a BA from Penn State University (We Are. . .). Mark lives with his wife in Shohola, PA, enjoys spending time with his family, and in his beloved Upper Delaware River Valley.

If you are interested in exploring franchise ownership or want to have a quick introductory conversation, please visit Mark at theperfectfranchise.com, or reach out to him directly at 973-452-4558 or mark@theperfectfranchise.com.

CPSIA information can be obtained
at www.ICGtesting.com
Printed in the USA
JSHW060431090623
42897JS00004BB/5